The SWEAT SHOP Book

CRAFTS & CAKES FROM THE PARIS SEWING CAFÉ

Ivy Press

First published in the UK in 2011 by
Ivy Press
210 High Street
Lewes
East Sussex BN7 2NS
United Kingdom
www.ivypress.co.uk

British Library Cataloguing-in-Publication Data
A catalogue record for this book is available from the British Library

ISBN: 978-1-907332-88-3

This book was conceived, designed and produced by
Ivy Press
CREATIVE DIRECTOR: Peter Bridgewater
PUBLISHERS: Jason Hook & Jenny Manstead
ART DIRECTOR: Wayne Blades
SENIOR EDITOR: Jayne Ansell
DESIGNER: Dominik Huber

Printed in Singapore

Colour origination by Ivy Press Reprographics

10 9 8 7 6 5 4 3 2 1

Both metric and imperial measurements are given throughout the book. To ensure accuracy of projects, the Sweat Shop team recommends you stick to one form of measurement throughout.

COVER PHOTOGRAPH:
Laurence Tarquin von Thomas, www.laurencevonthomas.com
Retouched by Tim Fahlbusch, www.timfahlbusch.com

TEXT:
Samantha Rajasingham

PHOTOGRAPHY:
Cassius, www.cassiusreel.com: p.124
Dominik Emrich, www.musiclies.com: p. 87
Esther Michel, www.esthermichel.com: p.147l
Histoire et vies du 10e arrondissement, www.hv10.org: p.12
Laurence Tarquin von Thomas, www.laurencevonthomas.com: p. 2, 13, 15, 16, 17, 70, 71, 127, 147r
Mélanie Petitqueux: p.8, 9, 20, 21, 45b, 53, 81, 136, 137, 138, 139, 150, 151
Munia Sbouri, www.muniasbouri.com: p.10, 25, 26, 27, 28, 29, 35, 36, 37, 38, 41, 42, 43, 44, 45, 46, 48, 49, 50, 51, 52, 57, 58, 59, 60, 61, 63, 64, 66, 67, 68, 69, 72, 74, 75, 76, 77, 83, 85, 86, 89, 91, 92, 93, 96, 97, 98, 99, 100, 101, 102, 103, 104, 105, 106, 107, 108, 109, 110, 111, 114, 115, 116, 117, 118, 119, 120, 121, 122, 123, 126, 131, 132, 135, 140, 141, 142, 143, 144, 145, 146, 148, 149, 156
Tanker, www.tanker.be: p.124, 125

TECHNICAL ILLUSTRATIONS:
Benedicte Flom: p. 80, 81, 82, 83, 84, 134, 135
Caroline Witzmann: p. 24, 25, 30, 31, 32, 33, 34, 54, 55, 56, 57, 62, 63, 132, 133
Emily Towers: p.126, 127
Isabell Thrun: p. 27, 39, 43, 47, 73, 90, 101
Madison O'Mara: p. 92, 93
Mlle Kou aka Céline Dupuy: p. 41, 42
Sébastien Davidtelevision: p. 88

MODELS:
Alison, Audrey, Bent, Céline, Charlie, Hubert, Isabell, Jade, Jazzmine, Kim, Lauren, Madison, Peter, Rain, Samantha, Tim

Sweat Shop would like to thank everyone who contributed to this book!

CONTENTS

PREFACE   7

SWEAT SHOP STORY   8

DO IT YOURSELF   20
COUTURE   22
KNITTING   78
CUSTOMIZE   94
DECORATION   112
TRICKS OF THE TRADE   128

RECIPES   138

SWEAT SHOP'S PARIS PICKS   150

GLOSSARY   158

INDEX   160

IF YOU HAVE THIS BOOK IN YOUR HANDS, OUR WORK IS ALMOST DONE. YOUR CURIOSITY HAS ALREADY BROUGHT YOU HERE, AND CURIOSITY IS HALFWAY TO CREATIVITY.

PREFACE

Sweat Shop – The Book is a sourcebook. It is a photo album full of inspiration because that's what Sweat Shop is: an inspiring place. The idea for our shop was to create a space where you can hire equipment, take classes in knitting and sewing, drink coffee and eat cake. However, putting people in touch with artists and master craftsmen gave rise to an unexpected variety of whimsical projects. People came back because Sweat Shop excited them; it is a crossroads for ideas.

This sense of community used to be familiar but can be hard to find in the city today. We thought about the little picturesque villages that our families are from. Not so long ago, it was common for people to get together to sew and knit. Friendships were nurtured over coffee and cake. We wanted Sweat Shop to re-create these villages.

We are located deep in the living heart of Paris, near Place de la République. Our little nook in the 10th arrondissement is truly one of the prettiest parts of the city. This is a place where young families mix with artists and the older, more established residents of the neighbourhood. People here are proud to be part of the new Paris; one that is not living in the shell of its past yet still retains its old-world charm.

Go ahead and turn the pages. Feel at home in our world. We hope this book is often in your hands, gets stained with coffee, folded with use. If that happens, we will be happy. And more importantly, we hope you will be, too.

Happy cake, coffee and crafting!

With love,

The Sweat Shop crew

www.sweatshopparis.com

SWEAT SHOP STORY

ONCE UPON A TIME, MARTENA, A MAKE-UP ARTIST FROM SWITZERLAND, AND SISSI, A FASHION DESIGNER FROM AUSTRIA, DREAMT OF A FUN PLACE THAT WAS BOTH A WORKSHOP AND A LIVING ROOM. THEIR COMBINED ENERGIES GAVE BIRTH TO SWEAT SHOP. IN THE COURSE OF ONE SHORT YEAR, MANY CREATIVE AND BEAUTIFUL PEOPLE HAVE WALKED THROUGH ITS DOORS. TODAY, 13 RUE LUCIEN SAMPAIX HAS BECOME A BUSTLING HUB FOR LIGHT-HEARTED PEOPLE JUST BRIMMING WITH INNOVATION AND WIT. THESE ARE PEOPLE WHO WEAVE TODAY'S PARIS INTO MACAROON COLOURS AND WHO HUNT FOR ADVENTURE IN HER LABYRINTHINE STREETS. WE ARE NESTLED NEAR THE MURMURING CANAL ST-MARTIN, AS IT WENDS ITS GENTLE WAY THROUGH THE CITY, OLD AND NEW. COME MEET OUR FAMILY. COME VISIT OUR HOME.

SWEAT SHOP GIRLS 10 OUR QUARTIER 14
THE 10TH ARRONDISSEMENT WALL OF FAME 18
– A SHORT HISTORY 12

SWEAT SHOP GIRLS

Martena (left) & Sissi (right)

THE GIRLS TOOK TIME OUT OF THEIR MAD HATTER SEWING PARTY TO ANSWER SOME QUESTIONS. HERE IS THE LOW-DOWN ON THE DYNAMIC DUO.

WHO ARE YOU?

Martena and Sissi. We are two expats who are based in Paris. Martena is a Swiss make-up artist who has called Paris her home for six years. Sissi, from Austria, previously ran Sissi Holleis in the 11th arrondissement, her own label and shop.

WHAT IS SWEAT SHOP?

A café couture, which means a coffee shop where you share ideas on sewing, and hire machines and materials to finish your projects.

WHEN DID YOU START SWEAT SHOP?

In November of 2009 a friend told us that there was a space opening up in the neighbourhood next to his shop. We started decorating in January, and by mid-March we opened the shop. It really only took four months for Sweat Shop to be born.

HOW DID YOU THINK OF IT?
WHAT TRIGGERED THE IDEA?

The idea came from remembering things past. We both come from communities where Sunday afternoon crafts and coffee are a regular thing. We love it, we missed it, so we decided to re-create it in Paris.

WHO VISITS SWEAT SHOP?

We get all sorts of people. Some of them are fashion students who do not have lots of space at home. Some of them are simply people who do not have a sewing machine. Others are people who have never touched a needle and thread in their life. We even get curious tourists who come in for cake and coffee.

HOW DO YOU EXPLAIN THE HYPE?

People have lost touch with making things by hand. Sweat Shop brings back the fun and satisfaction of making. It's more personal to make something and it slows time down. The move away from consumerism is a worldwide phenomenon, and we're part of this.

HOW IS SWEAT SHOP PART OF A NEW LIFESTYLE?

It's a way to socialize that is also very productive, rewarding and ultimately satisfying. And recycling is a way of life. Instead of buying, buying, buying, why not try to find a way to revamp your old clothes? It can be really fun and really creative. Even if you do not know how, we offer courses and professional help. And, when you make something, you're aware of the work and time you spent on creating that garment. It makes you proud.

PEOPLE SEEM TO BE LOOKING FOR A NEW 'HANDMADE, HOME-MADE' APPROACH.
WHY DO YOU THINK THAT IS?

We think it's great that the old stigma of 'home-made equals grandmother' is beginning to disappear. Just because we might use the techniques our grandmothers did does not mean we use them the same way. Websites such as Etsy do well because they tap into a love of adding a personal touch at home, and in life. After all, things that have been made with love last longer!

DOES EVERYONE GET THE JOKE IN THE NAME?
NO BAD REACTIONS?

Some people are offended by it, that's true. It was never intended to shock, but we do want to alert people to the issue; so yes, the name is definitely a comment on the whole cheaply produced throwaway situation that exists today. We think it's funny that people pay to sew in our Sweat Shop.

WHAT ARE SWEAT SHOP'S FUTURE PLANS?

We hope to open up more Sweat Shops, and therefore have fewer sweatshops.

THE 10TH ARRONDISSEMENT – A SHORT HISTORY

Le Pont Tournant de la Grange-aux-Belles, 1910

MANY THOUSANDS OF YEARS AGO, THE PLACE WHERE SWEAT SHOP NOW STANDS WAS A SWAMP.

Mosquitoes stung in summer and the natives, Parigi, paddled about in wooden canoes. The floodplain was rich in birds and beasts, and the various canals and creeks lent themselves to easy navigation by boat. It was from these humble beginnings that the great city of Paris was born, where civilization tamed the murky waters and built a glittering monument to all that was elegant, artistic and feminine in her soul. Today, no vestiges of her humble roots remain, except in the water that still runs through her.

The 10th arrondissement of Paris contains several important axes: the Gare du Nord, the gateway between England and France; the Gare de l'Est, opening the city up to the east and Germany; Place de la République, the very heart of Paris's Right Bank; and the Canal Saint-Martin. But all of these are recent additions. Before 1859, the 10th was not even considered a part of Paris. In medieval times it was unfortunately known for its insalubrious dwellings and its close proximity to the Montfaucon gibbet, now the picturesque Parc des Buttes Chaumont.

Le Pont Tournant de la Grange-aux-Belles, April 2011

The area we now consider the 10th owes its development first to the Hôpital Saint-Louis, erected in 1607 under Henry IV to relieve the workload at the Hôtel-Dieu. Its completion was shortly followed by a rise in the working-class population. In 1672 and 1674, two large triumphal arches were erected at the Porte Saint-Denis and Porte Saint-Martin by Louis XIV. Long boulevards were also added, making way for the bourgeoisie, who entered the 10th from this period onwards.

The nineteenth century saw the 10th blossom into what it is today. In 1825, by the original decree of Napoleon in 1802, the 4.5-km (2.8-mile) Canal Saint-Martin was inaugurated, linking the Seine to the north-west waterways and providing drinking water to the growing population. Twenty years later the two train stations were also built, and by 1859 the 10th was officially incorporated into Paris. The population exploded and was actually greater then than it is today.

One of the stranger stories of the neighbourhood is the theft in the early twentieth century of the *Mona Lisa*, originally thought to be a practical joke by Pablo Picasso and Guillaume Apollinaire. The *Mona Lisa* actually sojourned 28 months under a workman's bed on the Rue de l'Hôpital Saint-Louis. Vincenzo Peruggia, a Louvre glass-maker, lifted the *Mona Lisa* in 1911 and kept her until 1913, when she was forcibly removed from his premises.

Modern Paris shows her colours in the monuments and buildings that still tell her story. The area of the 10th remains working class, with a small mix of bourgeoisie, and it is a major interchange where those alighting from planes and trains first step into Paris. Heterogeneous and lively, the 10th of today is famous for its picnics by the canal, the small yet chic restaurants and its young designer boutiques. She's come a long way from her swamp days.

OUR QUARTIER

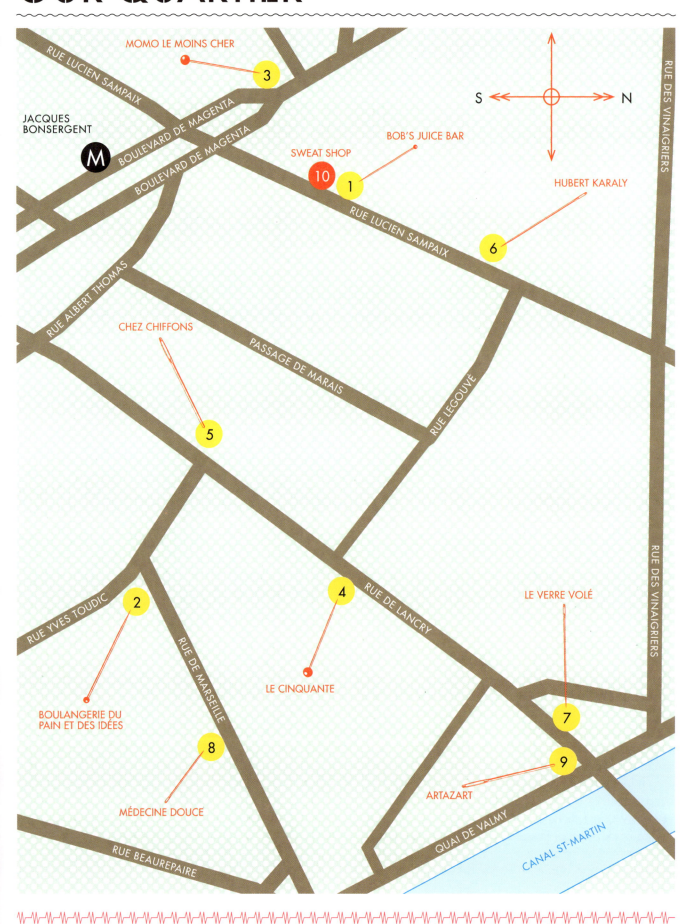

MOMO LE MOINS CHER

RUE LUCIEN SAMPAIX

3

S — N

JACQUES
BONSERGENT

M

BOULEVARD DE MAGENTA

BOULEVARD DE MAGENTA

SWEAT SHOP

BOB'S JUICE BAR

10 1

HUBERT KARALY

RUE LUCIEN SAMPAIX

6

RUE DES VINAIGRIERS

RUE ALBERT THOMAS

CHEZ CHIFFONS

PASSAGE DE MARAIS

RUE LEGOUVÉ

5

LE VERRE VOLÉ

RUE YVES TOUDIC

2

RUE DE MARSEILLE

4

RUE DE LANCRY

7

RUE DES VINAIGRIERS

BOULANGERIE DU
PAIN ET DES IDÉES

LE CINQUANTE

8

9

ARTAZART

MÉDECINE DOUCE

QUAI DE VALMY

CANAL ST-MARTIN

RUE BEAUREPAIRE

WELCOME TO OUR LITTLE VILLAGE IN THE 10TH. LOCATED BETWEEN PLACE DE LA RÉPUBLIQUE AND THE CANAL SAINT-MARTIN, THESE NARROW STREETS REFLECT THE BEST OF OLD AND NEW PARIS. A VIBRANT NEIGHBOURHOOD FILLED WITH ECCENTRIC BEAUTY, THE 10TH REPRESENTS MODERN-DAY PARIS WITH ITS MIX OF ETHNIC COMMUNITIES AND NEW BOHEMIANS. BY THE GLITTERING WATERS OF THE CANAL OR IN THE GRITTY GLAMOUR OF THE STREETS, TAKE A WALK IN OUR SHOES AS WE SHOW YOU THE 'HOOD.

1   BOB'S JUICE BAR
Soulful New Yorker Marc Grossman holds court at this lunch-box mecca. Sweat Shop's guardian angel is responsible for bringing cool to quinoa and often has off-day models rubbing shoulders with local folk. We love the muesli and can't say no to the bagels.

2   BOULANGERIE DU PAIN ET DES IDÉES
Being voted best baker by Gault Millau, the French restaurant guide, is no small feat, but what gets us coming back is the *pain des amis*, literally 'friends' bread'. With their creations ranging from little tasty fig and bacon rolls to apple strudels, we think you'll agree that they're tops.

3   MOMO LE MOINS CHER
Cheap! Cheap! Cheap! We don't want to sound like birds, but Momo's jeans, granny cardigans, Hawaiian shirts and rockabilly prints have us twittering with joy.

4   LE CINQUANTE

A real dive, thank the Lord! After a long day there's
no better place to get cosy with the natives than at our
local bar. There are even small oyster plates or cheese
and charcuterie to go with your wine and beer.
Warning: singing.

5   CHEZ CHIFFONS

This stylish hot spot is where we find vintage designer
clothes and upmarket treasures hand-picked by a
careful eye. Classic YSL silk blouses and gorgeous
Epoch shoes can be yours, for a price. This is one
mother's wardrobe we'd like to plunder.

6   HUBERT KARALY

Hubert. What to say about possibly the most striking
character on our street? What is his space? Is it a
gallery? Is it a country home? Is it another planet?
Well, it's the wonderful strange domain of Hubert
himself, who is one of the *grands hommes* of the
neighbourhood.

7   LE VERRE VOLÉ

This tiny restaurant is part of the new vanguard in the
Paris Le Fooding scene. Simple food, carefully sourced
ingredients, perfect cooking – chef Delphine Zampetti
rules the roost with her elegant yet unpretentious dishes.
Owner Cyril Bordarier stands firmly behind his rare
natural wines. You're sure to rub elbows with other
cognoscenti. Reservations necessary.

8 MÉDECINE DOUCE

Finely woven coloured bands and gold often make surprisingly graphic and textured jewellery. Many elegant strand effects that are definitely suitable for a young Cleopatra traipsing off to Milan to watch the opera. Sexy girl.

9 ARTAZART

Need some inspiration? Weekend strolls by the canal are not complete without a stop at this visual arts specialist bookshop. Chock-a-block with well-sourced contemporary photography and design books, the space also doubles as a gallery. Warning: you could be in there for hours.

1
BOB'S JUICE BAR
15 rue Lucien Sampaix
75010 Paris
www.bobsjuicebar.com

2
BOULANGERIE
DU PAIN ET DES IDÉES
34 rue Yves Toudic
75010 Paris
www.dupainetdesidees.com

3
MOMO
LE MOINS CHER
31 boulevard de Magenta
75010 Paris

4
LE CINQUANTE
50 rue de Lancry
75010 Paris

5
CHEZ CHIFFONS
47 rue de Lancry
75010 Paris
www.chezchiffons.fr

6
HUBERT KARALY
21–23 rue Lucien Sampaix
75010 Paris

7
LE VERRE VOLÉ
67 rue de Lancry
75010 Paris
www.leverrevole.fr

8
MÉDECINE DOUCE
10 rue de Marseille
75010 Paris
www.bijouxmedecinedouce.com

9
ARTAZART
83 quai de Valmy
75010 Paris
www.artazart.com/fr/

WALL OF FAME

OUR TOILET, ALREADY
WALLPAPERED WITH MEMORABILIA,
SETS THE SCENE FOR SOME OF
THE LOVELY PEOPLE WHO COME
SAILING THROUGH OUR DOORS.
HERE ARE SOME SNAPSHOTS
FROM THE ALWAYS EXCITING
SWEAT SHOP WORLD.

Ali Barrie, Montreal / model

Bent, Antwerp / musician & painter

Audray, Paris / gallerist

JP, Manchester / artist

Stéphane & Oliver, Paris / press agent & architect

Thomas, Paris / journalist

Lia, Paris / artist

Nevée, Paris / child

Amélie, Paris / actress

...ly, Brisbane / traveller

Claudia, Paris / all-rounder

Melanie, Paris / creative adviser

Claire, Paris / writer & teacher

Christina & Dominik, Zurich / journalist & designer

Rémi, Paris / musician

Filipe, Faro / community manager

Charlie, London / painter

Sarah, Stockholm / designer

Sam, Toronto / writer

Gaëtan, Ghent / photographer

Fred, Marseille / hairstylist

Irma, Prague / stylist

DO IT YOURSELF

DON'T BUY GRANDMA A PRESENT – MAKE SOMETHING ESPECIALLY FOR HER! FROM SEWN DESIGNER BAGS TO SPRAY-PAINTED SHOES AND ACCESSORIES, OUR GORGEOUS DO-IT-YOURSELF PROJECTS ARE EASY TO FINISH AND EXTRAORDINARY TO HAVE. THROWN INTO THE MIX ARE SOME DECORATING TECHNIQUES FOR CHRISTMAS AND CHILD-FRIENDLY PROJECTS JUST FOR FUN. WHILE SOME PEOPLE CALL IT INSPIRA-TIONAL, WE JUST THINK THAT BUSY HANDS MAKE LIGHT HEARTS. MAY THESE NEXT PAGES BRING A LITTLE SWEAT SHOP INTO YOUR HOME.

◤ simple ◤◤ medium ◤◤◤ advanced

COUTURE 22

THE SHOPPING BAG ◤ 24
*MAKE YOUR OWN
T-SHIRT PATTERN WITH
PELICAN AVENUE ◤ 26
ARABIAN SKORT ◤◤◤ 30
SEWING TOOLS 36
*THE MARTENA ◤◤ 38
ISA'S TWISTED HOODIE ◤◤◤ 42
*TODTI'S JACKET ◤◤◤ 46
TULIP DRESS ◤◤ 54
*MICHAËL VERHEYDEN'S
SHOPPING BAG ◤◤◤ 58
THE BANANA BAG ◤◤ 62
*SANDRINE'S FLAPPER
TROUSERS ◤◤◤ 64
MEET JADE 70
THE HOUSE BOOTIE ◤◤ 72
THE FAMILY HEADS
CHRISTMAS BAUBLES ◤ 76

KNITTING 78

THE QUICK-KNIT
FISHNET JUMPER ◤ 80
HOUSE SOCKS ◤ 82
THE KNITTED SNAKE ◤ 84
*SÉBASTIEN
DAVIDTELEVISION'S JUMPER
WITH A THEME ◤◤◤ 86
BALACLAVA ◤◤ 90
MADISON'S FINGER
PUPPETS ◤◤ 92

CUSTOMIZE 94

CROCHET CARDIGAN ◤ 96
MAKE YOUR OWN FABRIC ◤ 98
HESTER'S
PLAID-BLANKET CAPE ◤ 100
SLEEPING MASK ◤ 104
CUSTOMIZE YOUR
OLD SHOES ◤ 106
*VA-VA-VOOM JACKET ◤◤ 108

DECORATION 112

BONBON, DRAUGHT
BEGONE! ◤ 114
DELPHINE'S JEANS
MASK ◤◤ 118
*TANKER'S VINTAGE
WALL ◤◤ 124
*EMILY'S FLOWERPOT
COSY ◤◤ 126

TRICKS OF THE TRADE 128

A BALLSY PROJECT 130
WEAVING LEATHER 132
THE MAGIC PLAIT 133
LOOP KNITTING 134
THREADS: A PHOTO LOVE
STORY 136

*Masterclass sections are indicated in yellow throughout the book. These are special tutorials given by professionals who are regular collaborators with Sweat Shop.

FABRICS, PATTERNS AND COLOURS
GALORE – BASIC, INTERMEDIATE AND
ADVANCED PROJECTS TO GET YOUR
SEWING MACHINE HUMMING.

COUTURE

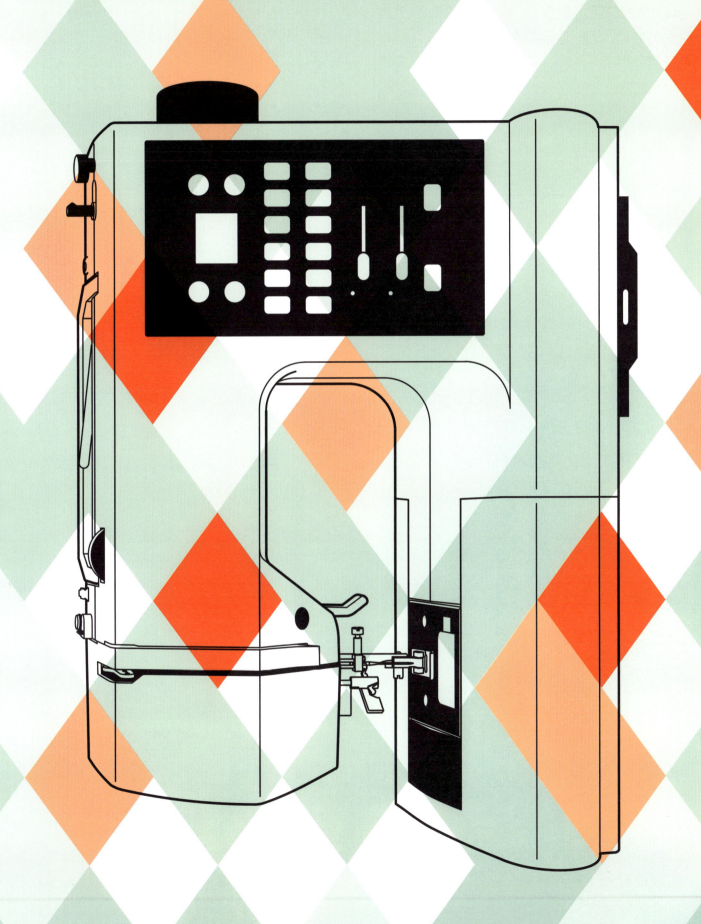

THE SHOPPING BAG

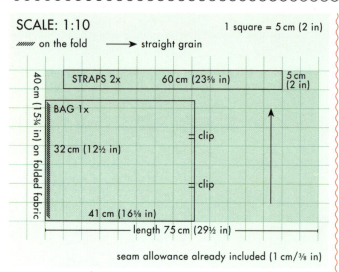

SCALE: 1:10

1 square = 5 cm (2 in)

〰️ on the fold   → straight grain

STRAPS 2x   60 cm (23⅝ in)   5 cm (2 in)

BAG 1x

40 cm (15¾ in) on folded fabric

32 cm (12½ in)

= clip

= clip

41 cm (16⅛ in)

length 75 cm (29½ in)

seam allowance already included (1 cm/⅜ in)

A SIMPLE BAG FOR SHOPPING, DRUMSTICKS, KNITTING GEAR, SPORTS KIT OR SMALL ANIMALS, YOU CAN SEW THIS EASY TOTE BAG IN AN AFTERNOON. USE EMBROIDERY, BUTTONS OR FELT-TIPPED MARKERS TO BRING BACK THAT INNER SCHOOL VOICE AND MAKE THIS BAG YOUR OWN.

What you need:
- fabric, 40 x 150 cm (15¾ x 59 in)
- bias binding, 62 cm (24½ in)

key: ─O─ right side / O─O wrong side

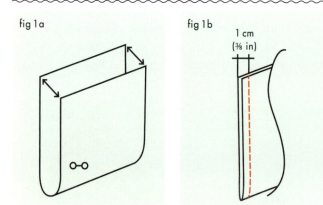

fig 1a

fig 1b   1 cm (⅜ in)

1 Fold the fabric in two (fig 1a), right sides together, and pin and stitch both sides closed allowing for a 1-cm (⅜-in) seam allowance (fig 1b).

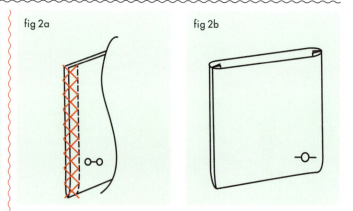

fig 2a

fig 2b

2 Overlock both sides (fig 2a) and turn the bag right side out (fig 2b).

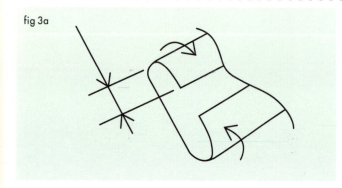

fig 3a

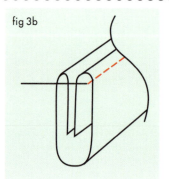

fig 3b

3 For the shoulder straps, fold 1 cm (⅜ in) of the long strap edges over to the wrong side (fig 3a), press, then fold the strap in half crossways and press again. Topstitch as close to the edge as possible (fig 3b).

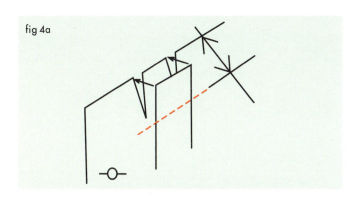

fig 4a

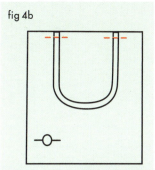

fig 4b

4 Place the short ends of the straps on the clips on the right side of the fabric. Stitch them across 1 cm (⅜ in) down from the top raw edge. (fig 4a,b)

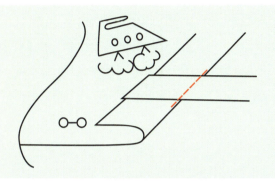

5 Fold over 1 cm (⅜ in) of fabric from the top edge of the bag to the wrong side and press flat.

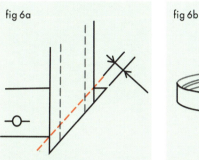

fig 6a

fig 6b

6 Unfold the bias binding and cut along the grain. The bias binding now has two parallel diagonal ends. Lay the bias binding, right sides together, perpendicular to itself with diagonal ends matching. Stitch the ends of the bias binding together, allowing for a 1-cm (⅜-in) seam allowance (fig 6a), and press the seam open. Turn the bias binding inside out and press the seam back into the folds of the bias binding (fig 6b).

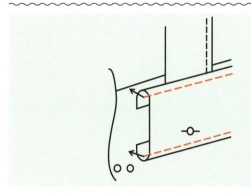

7 Pin the loop of binding on the inside of the bag, aligning the upper edge of the binding with the upper edge of the bag. Stitch along the top and bottom of the binding, 2 mm (¹⁄₁₆ in) from the edges.

MAKE YOUR OWN T-SHIRT PATTERN WITH PELICAN AVENUE

PATTERN MAKING, THE HOLY GRAIL OF SEWING, GETS DEMYSTIFIED. STARTING WITH A CROSS, PELICAN AVENUE SHOWS YOU, STEP BY STEP, HOW TO CREATE A PATTERN FOR THE EVERYDAY T-SHIRT. BY FOLLOWING CLEAR INSTRUCTIONS ON HOW TO GET PROPER MEASUREMENTS, AND DRAWING THEM EASILY ON SOME PAPER, WE HOPE THIS PATTERN-MAKING PROJECT WILL WHET YOUR APPETITE FOR THE TECHNICAL FINESSE OF COUTURE, AND HELP YOU PERSONALIZE THE SHAPE AND FORM OF THIS WARDROBE BASIC.

Carolin Lerch may have come from a fine pedigree of vintage fashion – her mother started one of the first vintage shops in Austria – but there's nothing old-fashioned about her. While her work may use textiles and knits, her prints and shapes are futuristic and she often collaborates with other contemporary artists. Also known under her artist persona, Pelican Avenue, Carolin is a conundrum. While her work refers to organic textures, she prefers using digital means to produce it. Her work is avant-garde, yet she loves old science-fiction films with static robots and tin foil heads. Whether she is creating new hybrid forms or holding performances where dancers are tangled in a web of knitting, her approach is multidisciplinary. Sweat Shop is delighted to count her among our satellites, a free electron moving in the sphere of pure creativity.

What you need:
– All tools are part of the sewing tools listed on page 36.

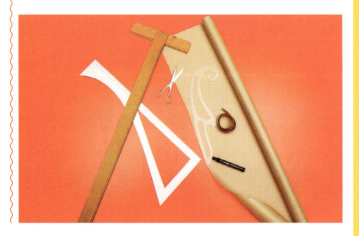

www.pelicanavenue.com

THE RULES OF MEASURING

Basic body measurements are needed to determine your pattern type and size. To get accurate body measurements, always use a tape measure and hold it flat and taut, without stretching. Standing up straight, with no shoes on, take all measurements from the same side of the body. TIP: Get a friend to help take the measurements.

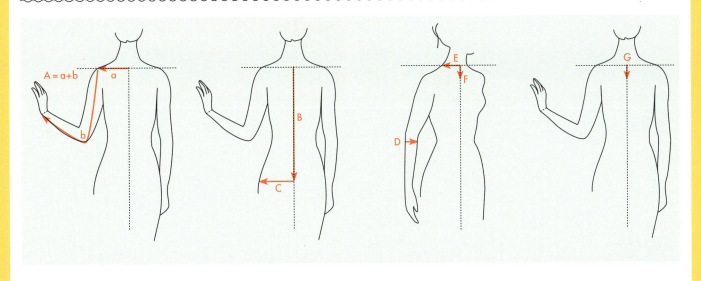

1

On a big piece of paper, draw a perpendicular cross in the middle. Mark your sleeve length on line A; mark your T-shirt length on line B.

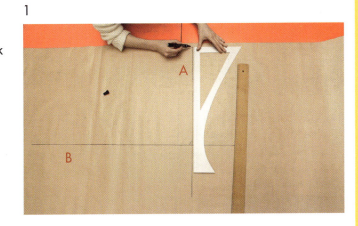

2

fig 2a

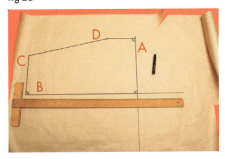

fig 2b

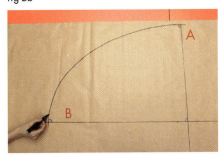

fig 2c

Mark the width of your shirt (C) and the width of your sleeve (D). How you connect the end points will change the shape of the T-shirt. For a more sporty silhouette, connect C and D with a straight line (fig 2a), for a bat-wing sleeve, connect A and B with a semicircle (fig 2b), for a classic T-shirt shape, connect C and D with an inner curve (fig 2c).

3

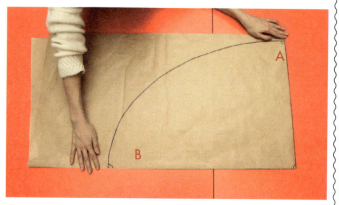

Fold the paper in four and cut along the A and B lines.

4

Cut out the rest of the pattern.

5

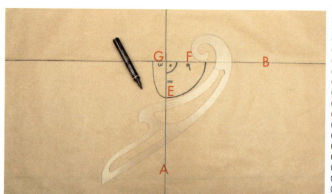

Unfold the paper. Draw the collar on the axis along B. Design your collar by choosing E (width of collar), F (front of collar) and G (back of collar). In the images, Carolin uses a standard measurement of 8 cm/3⅛ in (E), 9 cm/3½ in (F) and 3 cm/1⅛ in (G). Connect the three points with curved lines.

6

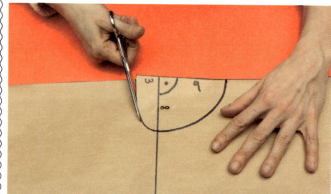

Fold the paper along B and cut out the circle of the collar.

THE RESULTS

Sporty shape

Bat-wing sleeve

Classic T-shirt shape

ARABIAN SKORT

ONE OF THE MORE CHALLENGING PROJECTS IN THIS BOOK, THE ELEGANT DRAPING OF THIS FEMININE SKORT TAKES ITS ORIENTAL CUE FROM *THE ARABIAN NIGHTS*. THIS PIECE OF EVENING WEAR IS CHIC ENOUGH FOR A DINNER PARTY, AND WILL TEACH YOU SOPHISTI-CATED SEWING TECHNIQUES SUCH AS HIDING ZIPS, MAKING FOLDS AND FINISHING A WAISTBAND.

What you need for a medium-sized skort:
- silk or cotton jersey, 2 x 1 m (76½ x 38¼ in)
- fusible canvas inter-lining, 20 x 40 cm (7⅞ x 15¾ in)
- invisible zip, 16 cm (6¼ in)
- zip foot

key: ⊸O right side / O⊸O wrong side

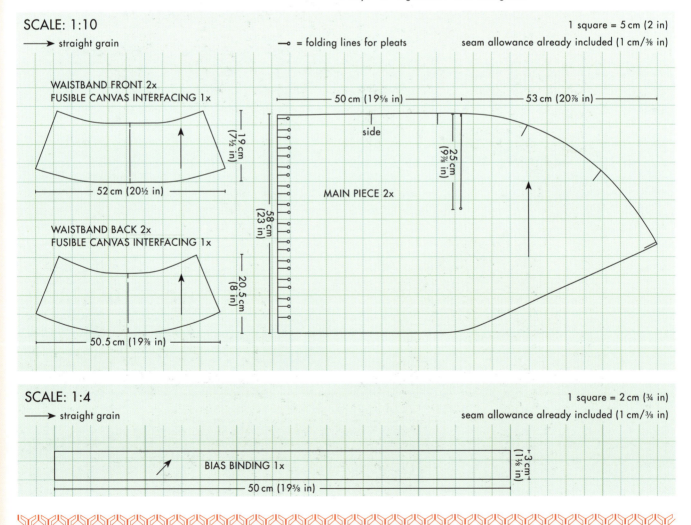

SCALE: 1:10

→ straight grain

⊸○ = folding lines for pleats

1 square = 5 cm (2 in)
seam allowance already included (1 cm/⅜ in)

WAISTBAND FRONT 2x
FUSIBLE CANVAS INTERFACING 1x

19 cm (7½ in)

52 cm (20½ in)

WAISTBAND BACK 2x
FUSIBLE CANVAS INTERFACING 1x

20.5 cm (8 in)

50.5 cm (19⅞ in)

50 cm (19⅝ in)

53 cm (20⅞ in)

side

25 cm (9⅞ in)

MAIN PIECE 2x

58 cm (23 in)

SCALE: 1:4

→ straight grain

1 square = 2 cm (¾ in)
seam allowance already included (1 cm/⅜ in)

BIAS BINDING 1x

3 cm (1⅛ in)

50 cm (19⅝ in)

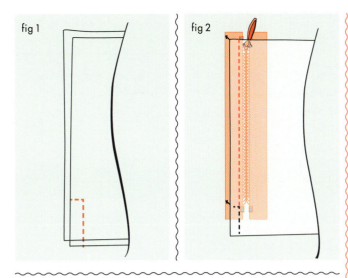

fig 1

fig 2

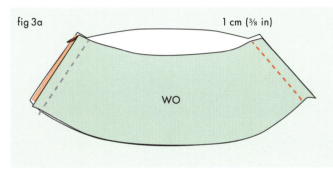

fig 3a

1 cm (⅜ in)

WO

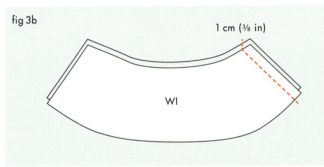

fig 3b

1 cm (⅜ in)

WI

1 Lay the pattern pieces on the fabric, pin in place, trace the folding lines and cut out. Each pattern piece is cut out twice, except for the bias binding, which is cut out once.

2 ASSEMBLING THE WAISTBAND: Cut the fusible canvas interfacing for the waistband – one front piece and one back piece. You should have two waistband front pieces and two waistband back pieces. Following the manufacturer's instructions, apply the fusible canvas interfacing to one of the front waistbands and one of the back waistbands. Note: The inner waistband (WI) has no interfacing, but the outer waistband (WO) does have interfacing.

3 Sew the invisible zip to the left side of the WO and close the other side of the WI and WO. For this, place the front of WO on the back of WO, right sides together, and stitch upwards 3.5cm (1⅜ in) from the bottom, allowing for a 1-cm (⅜-in) allowance (fig 1). Pin the left side and sew the zip as close as possible to the teeth of the zip (fig 2). Sew the right side of the zip on the back of WO. Sew the other side of the WO back and front piece together along the edge allowing for a 1-cm (⅜-in) allowance (fig 3a). Repeat for WI, right sides together (fig 3b).

TIP: Change the foot on your sewing machine to a special foot made for invisible zips.

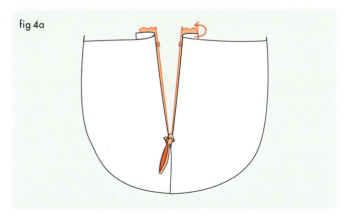

fig 4a

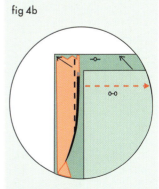

fig 4b

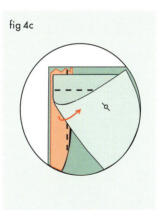

fig 4c

4 Now sew the top edge of WI and WO together (fig 4a). For this, pin the top edge of WO to the top edge of WI, right sides together, and stitch along the edge, allowing for a 1.5-cm (⅝-in) allowance (figs 4b/4c).

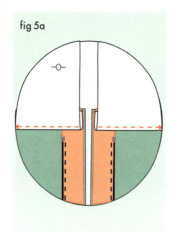

fig 5a

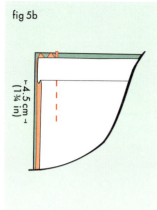

fig 5b

5 Flip WI up, press flat and topstitch along the edge, 2–3 mm (¹⁄₃₂–⅛ in) from the edge (fig 5a). Fold WI down and stitch 4.5 cm (1¾ in) down from the top edge, along the edge of the zip, allowing for a 1-cm (⅜-in) allowance (fig 5b). Stitch on the left and the right side of the zip.

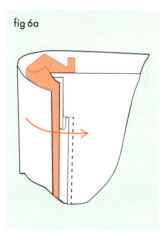

fig 6a

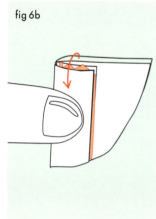

fig 6b

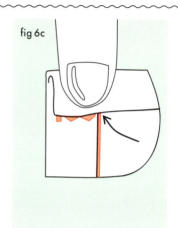

fig 6c

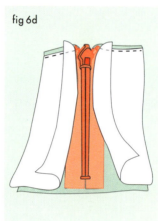

fig 6d

6 Turn the waistband inside out, starting with the corners of the zip, and push the corners to the point (fig 6a).

Press the corner down flat and push out the fold of the zip, keeping your thumb and forefinger on the corner (fig 6b). Then push out the top of the waistband (figs 6c/6d).

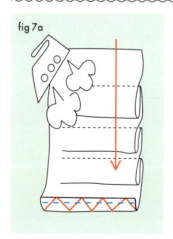

fig 7a

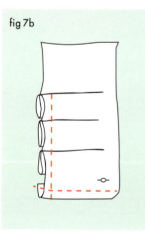

fig 7b

7 Overlock the bottom edge of the skort. Fold 5 mm (¼ in) of the hem to the wrong side, press and topstitch all along.

PREPARING THE PLEATS:
Place the fabric right side down. Make the pleats by joining the first folding line to the second folding line. Each pleat is 3 cm (1⅛ in) wide; the pleats are spaced 2 cm (¾ in) apart. Pin the pleats down, topstitch 1 cm (⅜ in) from the edge and press flat (fig 7a/7b). Repeat for both pieces.

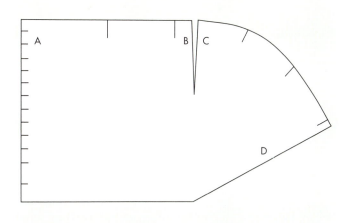

FINISHING THE SKORT: This key indicates the points in the two pieces that will be joined.

A1 = front middle, right side
B1 = back centre slit, right side
C1–D1 = beginning and end of three big folds that are placed on centre back, right side
A2 = front middle, left side
B2 = back centre slit, left side
C2–D2 = beginning and end of three big folds that are placed on centre front, left side

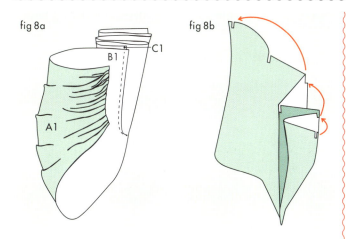

fig 8a

fig 8b

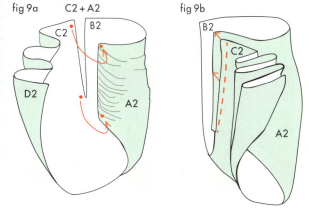

fig 9a   C2 + A2

fig 9b

8 Pin B1 to C1 and sew together, gradually decreasing from a 1-cm (⅜-in) to a 3-mm (⅛-in) seam allowance (fig 8a). Press the seam flat. Pin the pleats left between C1 and D1 along the folding lines. The first pleat starts 1 cm (⅜ in) from C1, and each pleat takes 23.5 cm (9¼ in) of fabric (fig 8b).

9 Bring A2 to C2 so that C2 lies on top of A2 (fig 9a). Pin and stitch them together allowing for a 1-cm (⅜-in) seam allowance, leaving B2 unstitched (fig 9b). Create the pleats as you did for step 8.

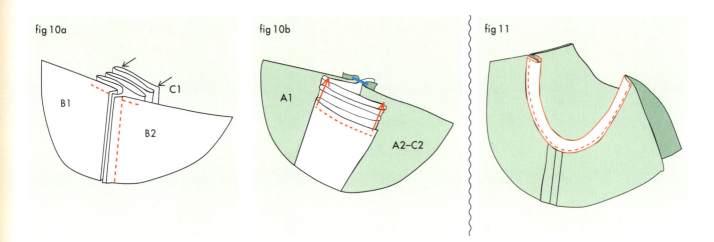

fig 10a

B1

B2

C1

fig 10b

A1

A2–C2

fig 11

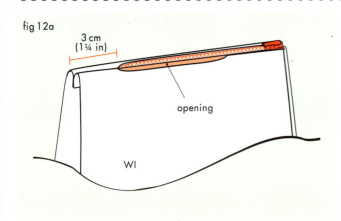

fig 12a

3 cm
(1¼ in)

opening

WI

10 Join seam B1–C1 to seam B2 and stitch, allowing for a 1-cm (⅜-in) seam allowance (fig 10a). Join A1 to C2–A2 and stitch, again leaving a 1-cm (⅜-in) seam allowance. There are three layers of fabric for each of these seams. Press the two pieces flat. Now lay the three folds on top of the waistband and stitch flat, leaving a 5-mm (¼-in) seam allowance (fig 10b).

11 FINISHING THE CROTCH:

Run the piece of bias binding around the inner seam of the crotch. There are six layers of fabric to wrap the bias around. Sew close to the edge (fig 11).

12 JOINING THE WAISTBAND:

Close WI by stitching 3 cm (1¼ in) along the length of the bottom of the zip, keeping the space along the rest of the zip open to pass the fabric through (fig 12a). Pin WI to the skort, right side facing wrong side, and sew, allowing for a 1-cm (⅜-in) seam allowance (fig 12b). Turn WO to the right side, pin and stitch on the right side of the previous seam, passing the fabric for the skort into the waistband as you go along. Stitch WO to WI along the same line as the stitch line for the skort. All the fabric is now inside the waistband (fig 12c). Pull the fabric through the hole in the zip and turn the garment inside out. Finish by hand-stitching the gap through which you passed the fabric closed.

fig 12b

WI

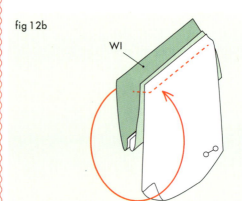

fig 12c

WI

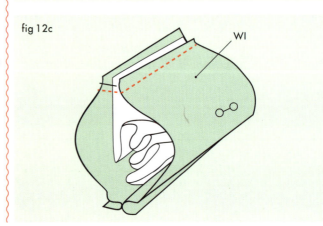

Sewing Tools

LIKE A MAGICIAN WITH HIS RABBIT AND TOP HAT, ANY GOOD NEEDLE-WORKER HAS THEIR BOX OF TRICKS. HERE IS A LIST OF EQUIPMENT WE LIKE TO KEEP CLOSE TO HAND. SOME OF THESE SUCH AS SCISSORS AND NEEDLES ARE BASICS THAT EVERY PROJECT WILL NEED. KEEP YOUR TOOLS IN GOOD CONDITION, KEEP YOURSELF ORGANIZED AND SEWING WILL BE A BREEZE.

1 Iron
2 Dressmaker's dummy
3 Ironing board
4 Pattern
5 Pattern paper
6 Embroidery scissors
7 Pinking sheers
8 Scissors
9 Pencil
10 French curve
11 T-square
12 Tailor's chalk
13 Plastic ruler
14 Seam ripper
15 Thread clipper
16 Bobbin
17 Thimble
18 Sewing machine foot
19 Sewing machine
20 Thread
21 Tape measure
22 Safety pin
23 Pins
24 Tracing wheel
25 Upholstery thread
26 Upholstery needle

THE MARTENA

THAT KOOKY MLLE KOU DESIGNED THIS HAT FOR OUR DEAR MARTENA. A BIT OF A FLOPPY THROWBACK TO THE '70S, THIS SASSY LITTLE NUMBER CAN BE THROWN ON FOR SUNNY AUTUMN DAYS OR SPRING FROLICS IN THE GARDEN. WE RECOMMEND WEARING IT WITH A NOD TO DIANE KEATON.

What you need:
- thick wool fabric or felt
  Brim: 45 x 120 cm
  (17¾ x 47¼ in)
  Crown: 20 x 120 cm
  (7⅞ x 47¼ in)
- ribbon, 70 cm (27½ in)
- ribbon and chain to decorate, 70 cm (27½ in) each
- button, 3 cm (1¼ in) diameter
- canvas fusible interfacing, medium weight, 45 x 90 cm (17¾ x 35½ in)

key: —O— right side / O—O wrong side

Céline Dupuy was once just a little girl who snuck up to her neighbour's flat to play with bright buttons, ruby ribbons and myriad scrap fabrics. It was from this early initiation into the world of couture that she found her love for colour and femininity. Every object she makes tells a story and she finds her inspiration everywhere – from people to feathers in the air. Already noted in France for her sewing book and pattern kits under her creative persona Mlle Kou, Céline believes that the new feminism is giving way to creative whims. She hosts a monthly workshop at Sweat Shop and enjoys exchanging ideas and meeting people through her work. She loves the colour peacock blue.

www.mllekou.com

1 square = 1 cm (⅜ in)

seam allowance already included (1 cm/⅜ in)

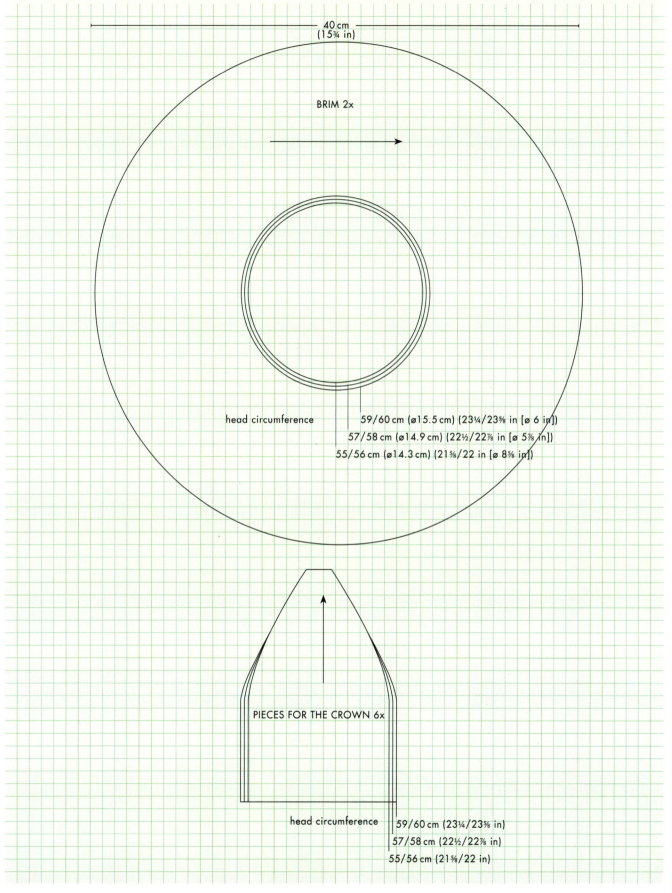

40 cm
(15¾ in)

BRIM 2x

head circumference

59/60 cm (ø15.5 cm) (23¼/23⅝ in [ø 6 in])

57/58 cm (ø14.9 cm) (22½/22⅞ in [ø 5⅞ in])

55/56 cm (ø14.3 cm) (21⅝/22 in [ø 8⅝ in])

PIECES FOR THE CROWN 6x

head circumference

59/60 cm (23¼/23⅝ in)

57/58 cm (22½/22⅞ in)

55/56 cm (21⅝/22 in)

1

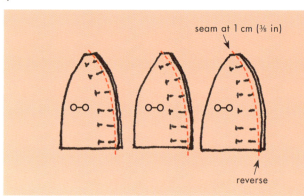

seam at 1 cm (⅜ in)

reverse

Measure the circumference of your head. Transfer the corresponding pattern piece on to pattern paper and cut out. Pin the six crown pieces for your size on to the fabric and cut out. Working in pairs, pin the pieces, right sides together, and sew, allowing for a 1-cm (⅜-in) seam allowance.

2

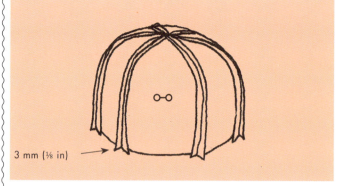

3 mm (⅛ in)

Sew the three pairs together, allowing for a 1-cm (⅜-in) seam allowance, to make the crown. Trim the fabric at the top of the seams.

3

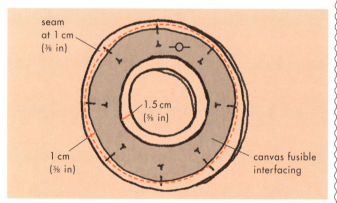

seam at 1 cm (⅜ in)

1.5 cm (⅝ in)

1 cm (⅜ in)

canvas fusible interfacing

Double the fabric, pin the brim pattern to it and cut out. Pin the pattern for the brim on the interfacing and cut out. Trim 1 cm (⅜ in) off the outer edge and 1.5 cm (⅝ in) off the inner edge of the interfacing. Following the manufacturer's instructions, apply the interfacing to the wrong side of one of the brim pieces. Pin the two brim pieces right sides together and stitch, allowing for a 1-cm (⅜-in) seam allowance. Press the seam and turn the brim right side out.

4

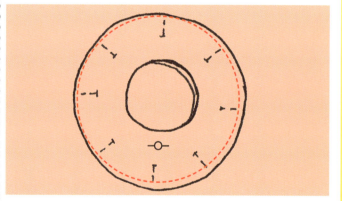

Topstitch along the edge of the brim, 5 mm (¼ in) from the edge.

5

a
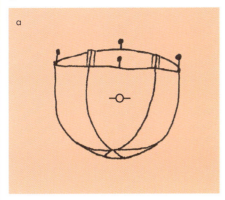

b
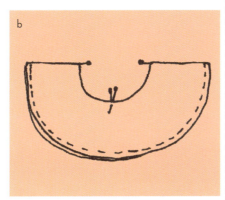

Mark four equidistant corners of the crown (fig 5a) and repeat for the brim (fig 5b).

6

seam at 1 cm (⅜ in)
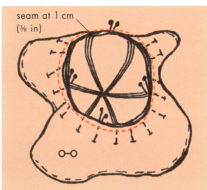

Match the marks and pin the two pieces together, right sides facing inwards. Sew, leaving a 1-cm (⅜-in) seam allowance. Press the inner seam flat against the crown.

7

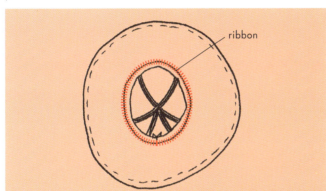

ribbon

Depending on the size of your head, sew a ribbon to the inside of the hat, over the seam that joins the crown and brim together. This ribbon can also be used to hide the stitching in the hat. Fix a button to the top of the crown. Measure out the circumference of the crown in chain and ribbon. Wind the ribbon either through the chain or around it. Stitch the ends of the ribbon together and close the links of the chain. Hand stitch the chain to the rim of the crown at a few points.

ISA'S TWISTED HOODIE

SHE IS NOT TWISTED BY NATURE, BUT HER HOODIE CERTAINLY IS. CONTRASTING COLOURS AND DIFFERENT FABRICS HELP BRING OUT THE PLAYFULNESS AND VERSATILITY OF THIS DESIGN. CHANGE YOUR MOOD – TURN IT INSIDE OUT.

Chances are when you first meet *Isabell Thrun* you'll find her rather timid and discreet. Then she stands up and you are struck by her height. Our resident Sweat Shop good fairy lets her creativity speak for itself. Blessed with many passions, she often marries her love of fashion with design and photography. Her début line featured multifunctional clothing made from softly draped, colour-blocked jerseys. It's not hard to imagine that her calm and gentle nature comes from hand-crafting things every day. Many bright and beautiful things wait in the wings for our young Isabell.

What you need for a medium-sized hoodie:
- two different rib knit fabrics, 120 x 120 cm (47¼ x 47¼ in)
- an alternate colour rib knit fabric for the bandings, 50 x 100 cm (19⅝ x 39⅜ in)

www.isabellthrun.de

ᨑᨑᨑ on the fold ⟶ straight grain

1 square = 5 cm (2 in)
seam allowance NOT included (1 cm/⅜ in)

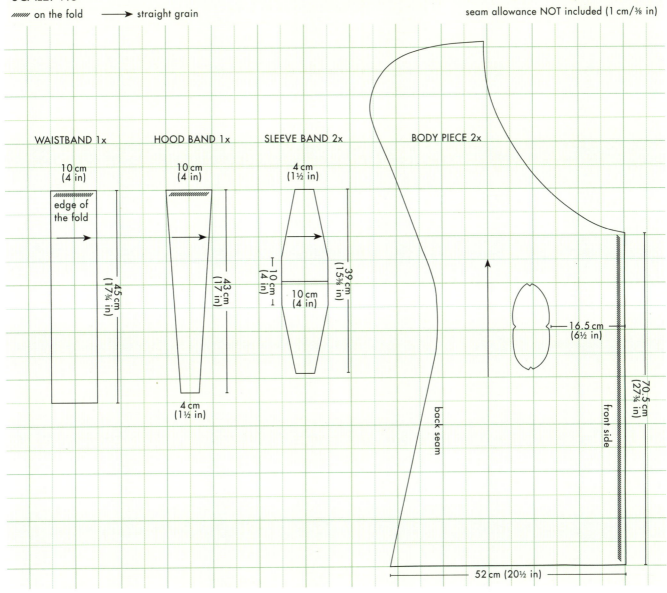

WAISTBAND 1x

10 cm
(4 in)

edge of
the fold

45 cm
(17¾ in)

HOOD BAND 1x

10 cm
(4 in)

43 cm
(17 in)

4 cm
(1½ in)

SLEEVE BAND 2x

4 cm
(1½ in)

10 cm
(4 in)

10 cm
(4 in)

39 cm
(15⅜ in)

BODY PIECE 2x

back seam

front side

16.5 cm
(6½ in)

70.5 cm
(27¾ in)

52 cm (20½ in)

1

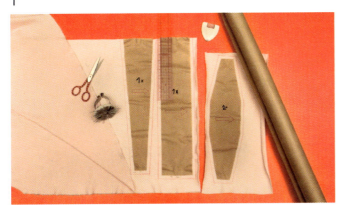

Fold the fabric and pin the patterns for the hood and shirt bandings to the edge of the fold, taking care to pin the pattern against the grain. Place the pattern for

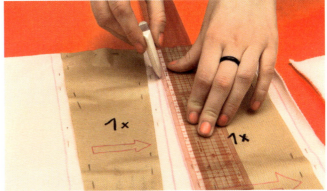

the sleeve band on the doubled fabric. Add a 1-cm (⅜-in) seam allowance all around all pieces, except along the fold. Cut the fabric out, but don't cut the fold.

2

Fold the fabric in two and pin the pattern for the waistband, hood band and sleeve band against the grain.

Add a 1-cm (⅜-in) seam allowance all around each piece, except along the fold, and cut the pieces out.

3

Pin the back seam of the body piece, right sides together, and sew it together using a zigzag stitch, taking care that the rib knit does not bunch up. Repeat for the second body piece.

4

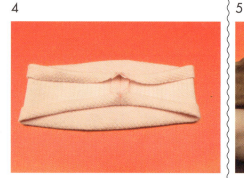

Sew the short ends of the sleeve bands, waistband and hood band together, right sides together, using 1-cm (⅜-in) seam allowances. Press flat.

5

Place one body piece inside the other body piece, wrong sides together. Pin the sleeve band on the edge of the sleeve fabric,

right sides together. Sew along the previously ironed fold mark of the sleeve band. Repeat with the other bandings.

6

Turn the shirt inside out. Pull the waistband fabric over the edges of the stitching, making sure that the fabric is equal on both sides, and secure with pins.

Baste evenly with red basting thread. Remove the pins and sew along the basting line, using thread that matches the fabric. Repeat for the sleeves.

Stitch the hood band by hand using an invisible stitch.

TIP: Change the thread often to prevent the banding unravelling should one thread break.

TODTI'S JACKET

HERE ARE INSTRUCTIONS FOR A BASIC WHITE JACKET WITH SLASH POCKETS, DOWN TO ITS FINEST DETAIL. THE CRISP CUT IS THEN ROUGHED UP WITH DYES AND PAINT. THE RESULT IS A VERY WILD TAKE ON AN OTHERWISE IMMACULATELY FINISHED PIECE.

Jörg Todtenbier, whom we affectionately call Todti, presides over Sweat Shop's couture masterclass. His attention to detail and excellent tailoring skills were honed at the internationally renowned Studio Berçot. With all that finesse, it's hard to believe that Todti got his start in fashion as a goth in Solingen, Germany. His hand-studded shoes and painted leathers soon had friends clamouring with personal requests. Today, Todti is in the process of starting an open space called Zweite Haut, dedicated to working on shapes in clothes. A firm believer in collaboration, Todti's generosity with time and instruction as well as his gleeful approach to colour are admired by us all.

www.zweitehaut.com

What you need for a medium-sized unisex jacket:
- any fabric:
  170 x 150 cm
  (70 x 59 in)
- elastic thread wound on a bobbin:
  100 cm (40 in)
- popper fastener tape
- facing tape
- design of your choice
- carbon tracing paper
- textile paint
- mechanical pencil

Set the sewing machine to a regular running stitch and turn the stitch length to 2.5–3 mm (about ⅛ in).

1 square = 5 cm (2 in)

seam allowance already included (1 cm/⅜ in)

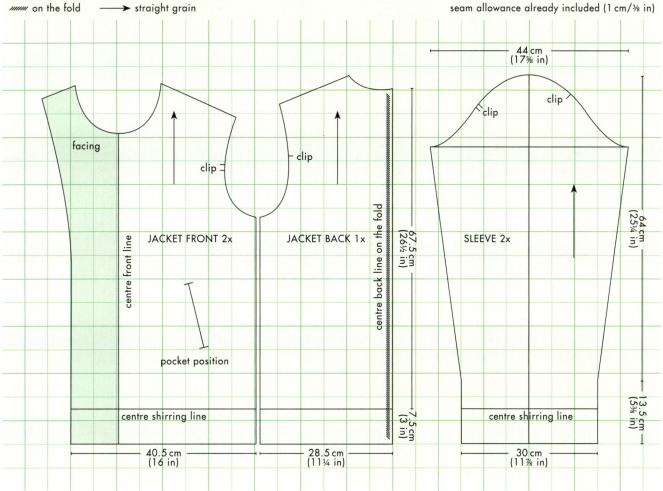

facing

JACKET FRONT 2x

centre front line

pocket position

centre shirring line

40.5 cm
(16 in)

clip

clip

JACKET BACK 1x

centre back line on the fold

67.5 cm
(26½ in)

7.5 cm
(3 in)

28.5 cm
(11¼ in)

44 cm
(17⅜ in)

clip

clip

SLEEVE 2x

64 cm
(25¼ in)

13.5 cm
(5⅜ in)

centre shirring line

30 cm
(11⅞ in)

SCALE: 1:3

~~~~ on the fold   → straight grain

1 square = 1 cm (⅜ in)

seam allowance already included (1 cm/⅜ in)

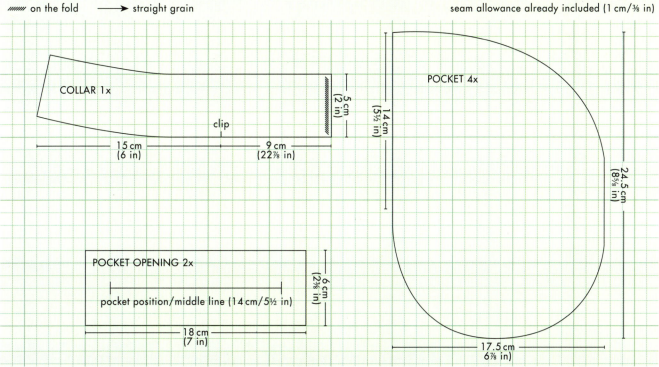

COLLAR 1x

clip

15 cm
(6 in)

9 cm
(22⅞ in)

5 cm
(2 in)

POCKET 4x

14 cm
(5½ in)

24.5 cm
(8⅝ in)

POCKET OPENING 2x

pocket position/middle line (14 cm/5½ in)

18 cm
(7 in)

6 cm
(2⅜ in)

17.5 cm
(6⅞ in)

1

Fold the fabric in two and take note of the grain. Place the pattern pieces on the fabric, respecting the straight grain arrow marked on the pattern, and trace your pattern with a pencil on the fabric.

2

Pin the fabric together at the corners and within the pattern outlines. Mark fold lines, darts and other markings with small clips.

3

Mark the position of the pockets with a pencil on the wrong side of the fabric. Prepare all pieces by overlocking the edges.

4

Mark the middle line on the two pocket openings and pin them to the right side of the jacket front pieces at the marked points.

5

Stitch twice around the pocket opening 2 mm ($\frac{1}{16}$ in) from the middle line. Repeat with the other pocket.

6

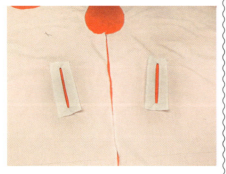

Cut along the middle line, working from the centre outwards. Cut a notch diagonally in each corner, taking care not to cut into the stitching.

7

Push the pocket opening pieces through the opening to the wrong side of the jacket fronts. Press flat.

8

Pin the pieces for each inside pocket on either side of the opening, right sides down.

9

Stitch again along the previously sewn pocket line.

10

Lay the pockets flat, pin along the edges and stitch along the curve.

11

Fold the edge of the facing 1.5 cm (⅝ in) to the left side of the fabric and topstitch, leaving a 1-cm (⅜-in) seam allowance.

12

Turn the facing to the inside and press flat.

13

On the bottom of the sleeves, mark three parallel lines every 2 cm (¾ in) above and three below the centre shirring line.

14

Thread your machine with cotton as the top thread and elastic thread wound on the bobbin. Shirr the first row and stretch the fabric flat when shirring all subsequent rows. Steam with an iron.

15

Pin the front and back pieces together at the shoulders, right sides facing, and stitch, leaving a 1.5-cm (⅝-in) seam allowance.

16

Pin the sleeves to the armholes, right sides facing, and stitch, leaving a 1-cm (⅜-in) seam allowance.

17

Fold the sleeves in half lengthways, right sides facing. Pin along the under-arm seam and the side edge of the body front and back pieces. Stitch, leaving a 1.5-cm (⅝-in) seam allowance.

18

Fold the lower edge of one collar piece over to the wrong side by 1 cm (⅜ in) and press. Aligning the top edges, pin the two collar pieces together, right sides facing. Stitch along the top edge and sides, allowing for a 1-cm (⅜-in) seam allowance. Leave the neck line open. Turn the collar right side out and press flat.

19

Fold the facing of the body along the centre front line, right sides together, and topstitch 1.5 cm (⅝ in) along the neckline, starting from the centre front, allowing for a 1.5-cm (⅝-in) seam allowance.

20

Aligning the raw edges, pin the unpressed, unstitched edge of the collar to the neckline, right sides facing, and stitch, allowing for a 1-cm (⅜-in) seam allowance.

21

Align and pin the collar's pressed edge to the neckline seam and stitch, leaving a 2-mm (¹⁄₁₆-in) seam allowance, or sew by hand using an invisible stitch.

22

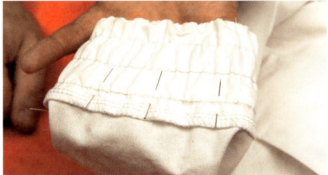

Turn the sleeves inside out, fold the cuffs back along the middle shirring line and pin in place. Stitch all along the edge of the cuff on the last shirring line.

23

Shirr the waistband as you did the cuffs, ending the shirring 8.5 cm (3⅜ in) from the centre front line.

24

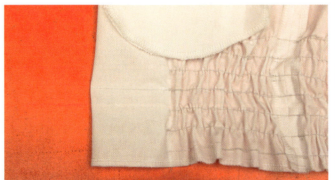

Fold the facing 8.5 cm (3⅜ in) of the body front piece along the centre front to the right side, right side facing, and stitch horizontally at 7.5 cm (3 in) from the bottom corresponding to the centre shirring line.

25

Fold the shirred waistband to the wrong side of the jacket along the middle shirring line and pin it to the facing of the front body piece and topstitch along the existing seam.

26

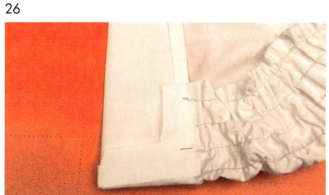

Turn the jacket inside out and trim the corner of the facing.

27

Turn the jacket right side out and fix the bottom by stitching along the edge of the waistband on the last shirring line.

28

Pin the facing to the shoulder seam and sew along the seam.

29

Pin the popper fastener tape to each side of the jacket. The male poppers should be on the inside, the female poppers on the outside.

30

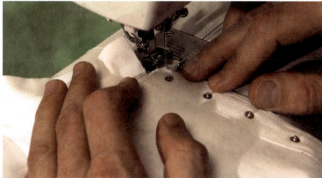

Using a zip foot on your machine, sew the popper fastener tape to the jacket along all edges of the tape.

Put on your jacket and try out different positions for your design.

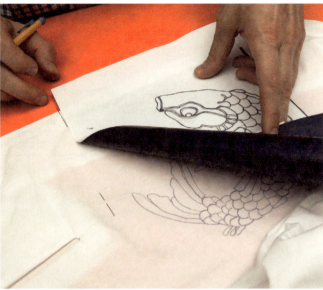

Place the jacket flat on the table, lay carbon tracing paper between the jacket and the design, and trace the design using a mechanical pencil with the lead retracted.

Start by painting the outlines. For the colour blocks try mixing the paint with water or other colours for texture.

◣ TULIP DRESS

WHO DOESN'T NEED A BILLOWING DRESS MADE FOR A DREAMY SUMMER DAY? HERE IS AN EASY PATTERN THAT CAN QUICKLY BE STITCHED TOGETHER. BEST WORN FOR PRETTY PROMENADES AND ALL THOSE ROMANTIC MEETINGS ON THE TERRACE.

What you need for a medium-sized dress:
- light jersey, thin cotton or silk, 1.5 x 1m (58½ x 40½ in)
- elastic band, 80cm x 5mm (31 in x ¼ in)
- optional lace, 1m (40½ in)

key: ○— right side / ○—○ wrong side

SCALE: 1:10

〰 on the fold　　→ straight grain　　○—○ = folding lines for pleats

1 square = 5 cm (2 in)

seam allowance already included (1 cm/⅜ in)

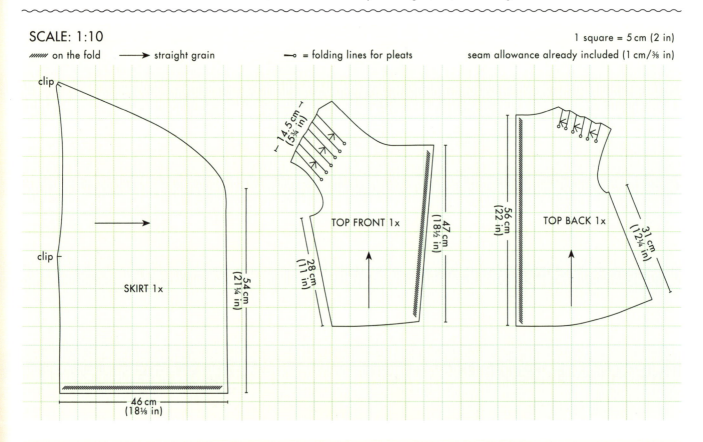

clip

clip

SKIRT 1x

54 cm (21¼ in)

46 cm (18⅛ in)

14.5 cm (5¾ in)

TOP FRONT 1x

47 cm (18½ in)

28 cm (11 in)

56 cm (22 in)

TOP BACK 1x

31 cm (12¼ in)

SCALE: 1:4

〰 on the fold　　→ straight grain

1 square = 2 cm (¾ in)

seam allowance already included (1 cm/⅜ in)

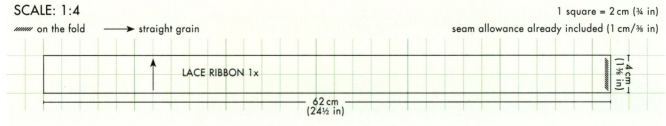

LACE RIBBON 1x

62 cm (24½ in)

4 cm (1⅜ in)

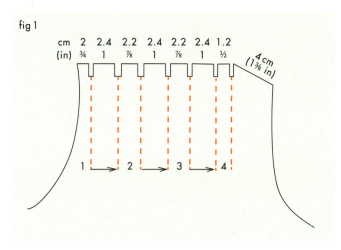

fig 1

| cm | 2 | 2.4 | 2.2 | 2.4 | 2.2 | 2.4 | 1.2 |
| (in) | ¾ | 1 | ⅞ | 1 | ⅞ | 1 | ½ |

4 cm (1⅜ in)

1 → 2 → 3 → 4

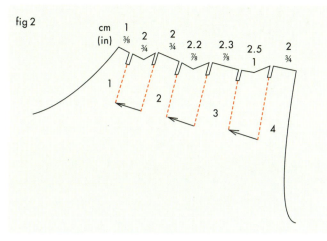

fig 2

| cm | 1 | 2 | 2 | 2.2 | 2.3 | 2.5 | 2 |
| (in) | ⅜ | ¾ | ¾ | ⅞ | ⅞ | 1 | ¾ |

1 2 3 4

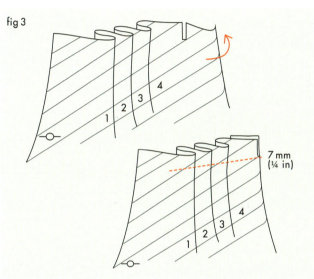

fig 3

4
2 3
1

7 mm (¼ in)

1 2 3 4

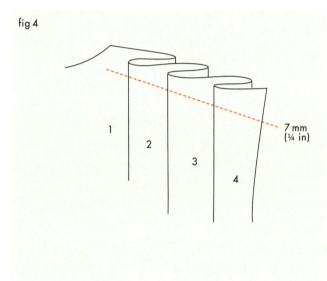

fig 4

1
2
3
4

7 mm (¼ in)

1 Overlock each fabric piece. Fold the front shoulder pleats (fig 1), and the back shoulder pleats (fig 2). Fold over the fabric after the lip, wrong sides facing (fig 3). Stitch lengthways, across the pleats, leaving a 7-mm (¼-in) seam allowance (fig 4).

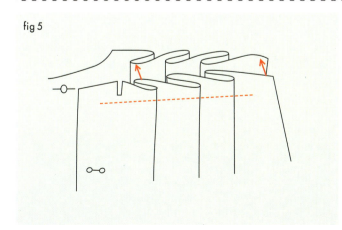

fig 5

2 Place the two shoulder pieces together, right sides facing, fold on top of fold, and stitch, leaving a 1-cm (⅜-in) seam allowance (fig 5).

fig 6

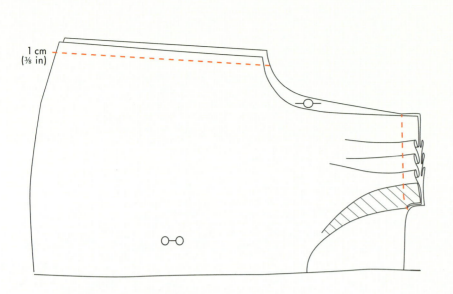

1 cm
(⅜ in)

3 Right sides facing, pin and stitch the sides of the bodice, leaving a 1-cm (⅜-in) seam allowance (fig 6).

4 Overlock the edges of the neckline, the armhole and the hem of the skirt. Fold the hem up 7 mm (¼ in) and stitch along the edge 5 mm (³/₁₆ in) from the fold (fig 7).

fig 7

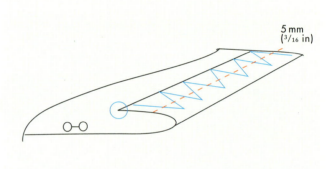

5 mm
(³/₁₆ in)

fig 8

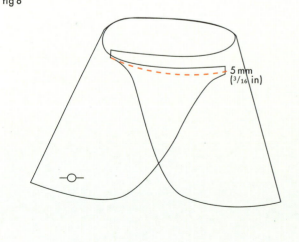

5 mm
(³/₁₆ in)

5 Wrap the skirt closed, lining up the folding lines, and stitch along the overlapped section of fabric with a 5-mm (³/₁₆-in) seam allowance (fig 8).

fig 9

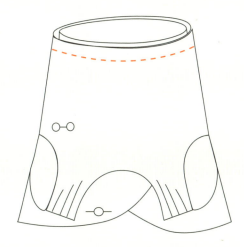

fig 10

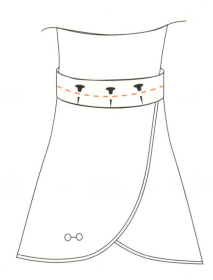

6 Lay the skirt inside the tube of the bodice, right sides together. Pin and then stitch all along the edge, allowing for a 1-cm (⅜-in) seam allowance (fig 9).

7 Pin the elastic around the seam joining the bodice and the skirt. Stitch along the centre seam, pulling the elastic as you go so that the fabric lies flat (fig 10).

TIP: TO MAKE YOUR DRESS MORE ATTRACTIVE AND GIVE IT A LIGHT ROMANTIC TOUCH, ADD A LACE BAND ON THE OUTSIDE, RUNNING ALONG THE WAISTBAND.

MICHAËL VERHEYDEN'S SHOPPING BAG

MICHAËL'S METICULOUS ATTENTION TO DESIGN AND FINISHING DETAILS ARE HIGHLIGHTED IN THIS BRILLIANT BAG. USING TRADITIONAL SADDLERY TECHNIQUES, HIS BAG FEATURES PROFESSIONAL LEATHER STITCHING AND A THOROUGHLY MODERN SHAPE. WE THINK MICHAËL'S BAG IS A BOLD STATEMENT IN URBAN ELEGANCE.

What you need:

- coated waterproof fabric, a firm fabric works best, 120 x 80 cm (47¼ x 31½ in)
- leather or strong fabric for the straps, two pieces 65 x 1.5 cm (25½ x ⅝ in) depending on your desired length
- leather paint (ask a shoe repair shop)
- waxed linen thread
- awl
- silver ink pen or chalk
- leather needles for hand stitching
- two metal clips
- snap-off knife
- card pattern of your choice (Michaël makes his initials MV); this pattern not only serves as a decoration, but also fixes the hem on both sides
- an old T-shirt or apron to protect your clothes from the paint

Michaël Verheyden's whole ethos is based on formal purity mixed with absolute functionality. This mathematical sensualist will be the first to admit that the process of making is where he finds his peace. Finding that Sweat Shop shared his brand of creativity, he came by to host a workshop. There he shared some of his trade secrets and conveyed his passion for the silent object: every detail must have its reason, every line must have its purpose, but none must dominate the whole. Though his objects present a calm facade, Michaël himself is always restless with new concepts.

Taken under the wing of Raf Simons early in his career, Michaël has been running his own design company since 2002. His work has received numerous accolades, notably from *Wallpaper* magazine.

www.michaelverheyden.be

1

Using the pen or chalk, trace a 2:1 main piece of 120 x 60 cm (47¼ x 23⅝ in) and a smaller piece of 20 x 50 cm (7⅞ x 19⅝ in) on your coated fabric.

2

Cut a straight line using a ruler and snap-off knife.

3

Fold the main piece into an M shape, right sides together. The folded bag should now be about 50 cm (19⅝ in) long, with a 10-cm (4-in) fold.

4

Close the sides of the bag by stitching all along both sides, the width of the foot on your sewing machine from the edge.

5

Turn the bag inside out. The clever folded bottom corners of this design are now visible.

TIP: WITH LEATHER YOU USUALLY DON'T USE PINS. EITHER USE GLUE TO FIX THE POCKET IN PLACE BEFORE YOU STITCH OR SEW IT ON AND THEN CLEAN UP THE EDGES WITH A NEAT CUT NEAR THE STITCHING LINE.

6

For the inside pocket fold the small piece of fabric as shown or as desired. Make sure that the flap is at least 12 cm (4¾ in).

7

Join the sides of the pocket together by stitching all along both sides, the width of the foot on your sewing machine from the edge.

8

Attach the inside pocket to the bag by simply stitching the pocket, opening facing down, to the right side of the bag, 10 cm (4 in) from the edge.

9

For the hem measure 5 cm (2 in) from the edge.

10

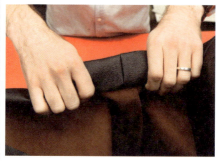

Fold the hem over twice. The hem takes 10 cm (4 in) off the top of your material.

11

Use the metal clips to hold the hem down and mark the holes of your prepared pattern on the sides of the bag.

12

Use the awl to make the marked holes. This can be quite difficult since there is a lot of fabric.

13

Using two needles and the waxed linen thread, pull the thread through the first hole, making sure both ends are the same length. TIP: To make it easier to thread the needle, flatten the thread with your fingernails.

14

Stitch your design, going twice through each hole to make it even stronger. This functional yet decorative technique is particular to stitching saddles. Finish your stitch between the fabric layers to hide the knot.

15

For the straps of the bag, Michaël uses prepared leather straps. You can replace this with leather or strong fabric; cut two pieces of the desired length or 65 x 1.5 cm (25½ x ⅝ in).

16

Paint the edges of your fabric or leather with leather paint. Using an apron is recommended at this point. Leave to dry.

17

Use the awl to make 4 to 6 holes on both ends of your straps.

18

Make the same holes on the bag, staying within the hem and remaining equidistant from the sides.

19

Attach the strap to the bag with the linen thread, using the same saddle stitch as before. If done correctly there are two crosses in the back and three equal stripes on the front.

20

End your stitch between fabric layers for a clean finish.

21

Feeling ambitious? Make a little keychain by cutting another piece of leather as shown and attach it to the bag.

THE BANANA BAG

THE BANANA BAG, THAT MALIGNED MAINSTAY OF THE '80S, GETS A MAKEOVER. ITS ECCENTRICITY HAS BEEN CELEBRATED AND SCORNED BY STYLISTS AND FASHIONISTAS ALIKE. HERE AT SWEAT SHOP, WE MADE A FEMININE AND LIGHTWEIGHT VERSION THAT IS AS PRACTICAL AS IT IS BEAUTIFUL. ON THE ROAD WITH THE GLOBETROTTER AND SPOTTED IN CLUBS, THE BANANA BAG IS A MUST FOR THOSE WHO WANT TO KEEP THEIR HANDS FREE AND THEIR LOOK FRESH. ADAPTABLE FOR MEN BY USING A STURDIER MATERIAL SUCH AS LINEN OR DENIM.

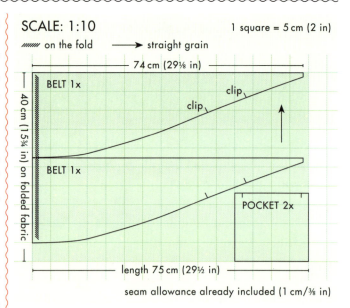

SCALE: 1:10 1 square = 5 cm (2 in)

〰 on the fold → straight grain

74 cm (29⅛ in)

BELT 1x

40 cm (15¾ in) on folded fabric

clip   clip
clip

BELT 1x

POCKET 2x

length 75 cm (29½ in)

seam allowance already included (1 cm/⅜ in)

What you need:
- silk fabric, 50 x 150 cm (19⅝ x 59 in)
  TIP: You could recycle some old silk scarves.
- invisible zip, 16 cm (6¼ in)
- zip foot

key: ─O─ right side / O─O wrong side

fig 1a

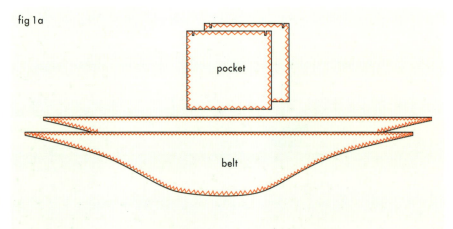

pocket

belt

fig 1b

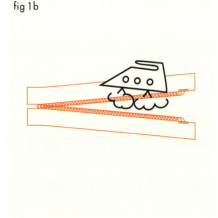

1 Overlock all the edges of the belt and pocket pieces (fig 1a).

Open the zip and press flat (fig 1b).

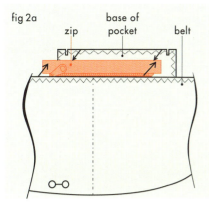

fig 2a — zip / base of pocket / belt

2 Pin the zip between the edge of the pocket piece and the belt (fig 2a).

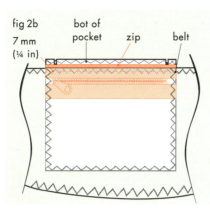

fig 2b — 7 mm (¼ in) / bot of pocket / zip / belt

Using the zip foot, push the machine needle to the left side and sew, leaving a 7-mm (¼-in) seam allowance (fig 2b). Repeat on the other side.

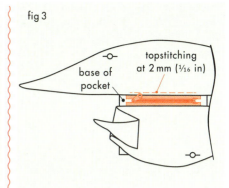

fig 3 — base of pocket / topstitching at 2 mm (¹⁄₁₆ in)

3 Lay the work flat, pull the pocket to the other side and topstitch 2 mm (¹⁄₁₆ in) from the edge of the belt. Repeat on the other side.

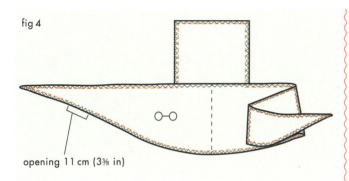

fig 4 — opening 11 cm (3⅜ in)

4 Sew the pocket, right sides together, leaving a 1-cm (⅜-in) seam allowance, then sew the two tops of the belt on both sides of the zip. Sew all around the edges of the belt, leaving a 1-cm (⅜-in) seam allowance. Keep an opening of 11 cm (3⅜ in) to turn the bag right side out.

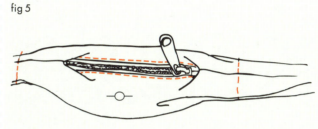

fig 5

5 Turn the bag right side out. Fold under the raw edges of the opening to the wrong side and stitch 2 mm (¹⁄₁₆ in) from the edge to close the gap. Mark a point 50 cm (20 in) in from the end of the belt. At this point push the fabric inwards, on both sides, to a depth of 2.5 cm (1 in) to create folds, and press flat. Stitch a line perpendicular to the length of the belt to hold the folds in place.

SANDRINE'S FLAPPER TROUSERS

IN THIS PROJECT, OUR EMBROIDERY EXPERT SANDRINE USES SILK PAPER AS A STABILIZER TO HELP FIX THE LACE TO THE FABRIC. THE SHAPE OF THESE OVERALLS IS WITTILY MIRRORED IN THE BANANA INSETS. THE REMARKABLE FLUIDITY AND GENTLE, FLATTERING SHAPE ARE EASILY ACHIEVED USING A MIXTURE OF MATERIALS AND TECHNIQUES. OUR FAVOURITE PART ABOUT THIS PROJECT IS THAT IT FEATURES FOUR IDENTICAL MAIN PIECES, MAKING IT REMARKABLY EASY TO CRAFT.

Sandrine Doczekalski has the poise and elegance of a *grande dame*, but she giggles like a girl. Her joyful approach to fashion is above all feminine and chic, with a few bananas thrown in. In charge of accessories and sunglasses at Sonia Rykiel, flashes of punk rock and Josephine Baker run through her work. Inspiration for this Parisienne comes from the change in seasons, the sun on the walls of her neighbour's home and the textures of fruits and flowers. Her work uses everything from plastic to stone to create unexpected lines and volume. At her masterclass in embroidery, clients always marvel at her good humour and her unfailing good taste. She shared with us a little secret: being beautiful and intelligent today is understanding what you need and knowing you have the means to make it happen. We understand what this fine young lady is talking about.

What you need:
– lace
– silk cotton, 350 x 150 cm
  (138 x 59 in)
– silk paper

princesstamdam.blogspot.com

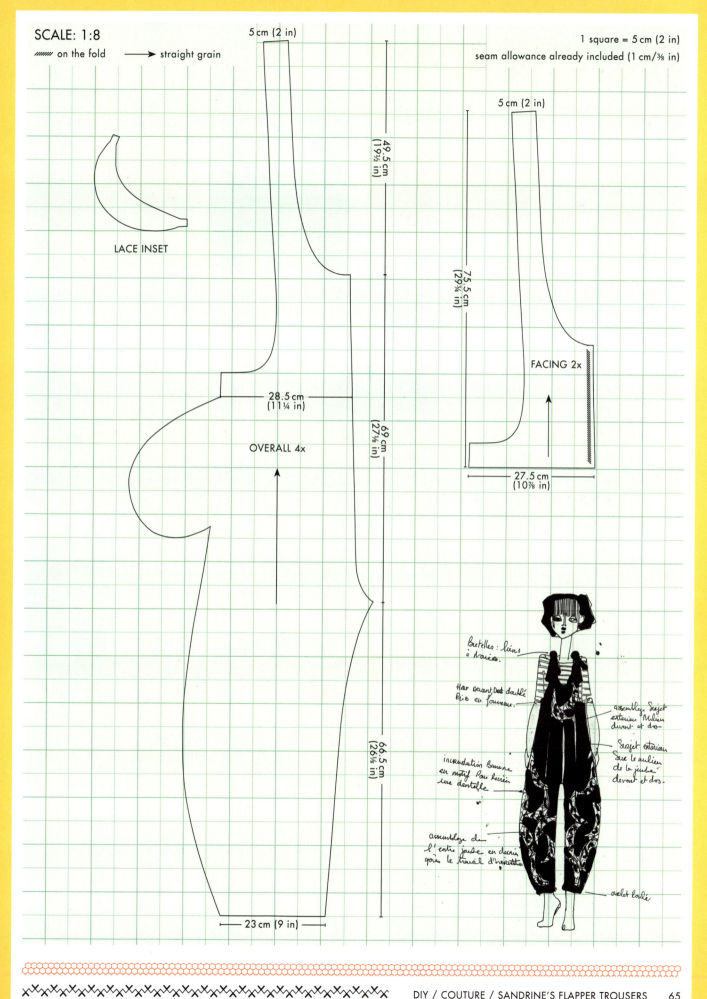

SCALE: 1:8

〰〰 on the fold ⟶ straight grain

5 cm (2 in)

1 square = 5 cm (2 in)
seam allowance already included (1 cm/⅜ in)

5 cm (2 in)

LACE INSET

49.5 cm
(19½ in)

75.5 cm
(29¾ in)

FACING 2x

28.5 cm
(11¼ in)

69 cm
(27⅛ in)

OVERALL 4x

27.5 cm
(10⅞ in)

66.5 cm
(26⅛ in)

23 cm (9 in)

1

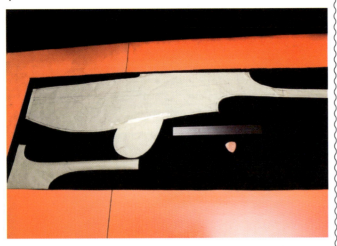

Fold your fabric, rights sides together, and pin the pattern pieces on top. Place the facing on the fold of the fabric.

2

Use chalk to mark out the outline of the pattern.

3

Pin the layers of fabric together and cut out. Repeat steps 1–3 to make four identical pieces for the legs.

4

Stitch two of the four main pieces, right sides together, down the centre. Repeat with the remaining two pieces. Now you have the front and the back pieces.

5

Overlock the bottom edge of the facings. Pin the facings to the straps, right sides together, and stitch all along the curves of the straps, leaving a 1-cm (⅜-in) seam allowance. Do not stitch the sides.

6

Trim the seams on the straps to half their width and snip the corners of the straps, taking care not to cut through the stitches. Turn the straps right side out and press flat. Simply tidy up the ends of the straps before wearing your finished trousers.

7

Cut out squares of lace and silk paper for the bananas. Prepare as many of these squares as you need for the number of banana insets you want.

8

Place the banana pattern on the top of the fabric, right side facing up. Place the layers of lace and paper underneath and pin together. Trace the outline of the banana. Fix all three layers together carefully by sewing along the edges of the banana with a satin stitch 2–3 mm (about ¹⁄₁₆ in) in width.

9

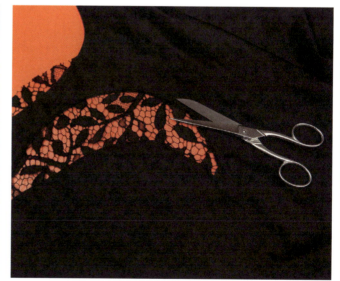

Tear off the paper. Use a pair of scissors to carefully cut away the fabric inside the banana shape, taking care not to cut through any seams or lace.

10

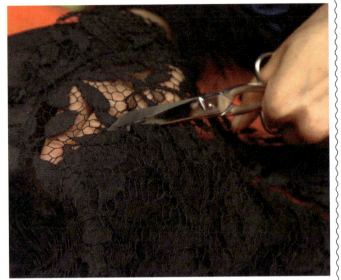

Turn the piece over and trim off the edges of the lace, leaving about 2 mm (1/16 in) of lace around the outline. Press flat. Repeat steps 8–10 for all the remaining banana insets.

11

Place the two main pieces, right sides together, on top of each other. Pin along the edges and the crotch and stitch.

12

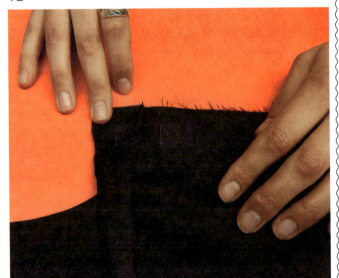

Flip the facing over the waistband of the side seam, pin together and stitch, leaving a 1-cm (3/8-in) seam allowance. Overlock to finish the edges of the seam.

13

Finish the trouser hem by either overlocking or hemming.

MEET JADE, OUR 10-YEAR-OLD
COUTURE STAR. A SWEAT SHOP
REGULAR, THIS LITTLE MISS HAS
ALREADY DESIGNED HER VERY
OWN SWEAT SHOP COLLECTION.
WE CAN BARELY WAIT TO SEE
WHAT THIS PINT-SIZED TORNADO
OF CREATIVITY MAKES NEXT.

THE HOUSE BOOTIE

KEEP YOUR FAMILY'S PRECIOUS FEET WARM AND FASHIONABLE IN THESE ADORABLE HOME-MADE HOUSE BOOTIES. THE BOOTIES ARE A FUN AND EASY WAY TO USE SCRAP FABRIC. IF YOU HAVE CHILDREN, YOU MAY FIND YOURSELF SAVING LOTS OF MONEY WHEN THEIR FEET GROW. ADD LITTLE PERSONAL EMBELLISHMENTS SUCH AS EMBROIDERY OR CLOTH PAINT FOR THAT BOOTILICIOUS TOUCH.

What you need:
- outer shell: any sturdy fabric (old jeans, felt, sturdy cotton), 30 cm (12 in)
- lining: soft and thick breathable fabric (velvet, padded cotton), 30 cm (12 in)
- leather pieces for the sole
- elastic band, 2 x 6 cm (¾ x 2⅜ in)

〰〰 on the fold　──→ straight grain

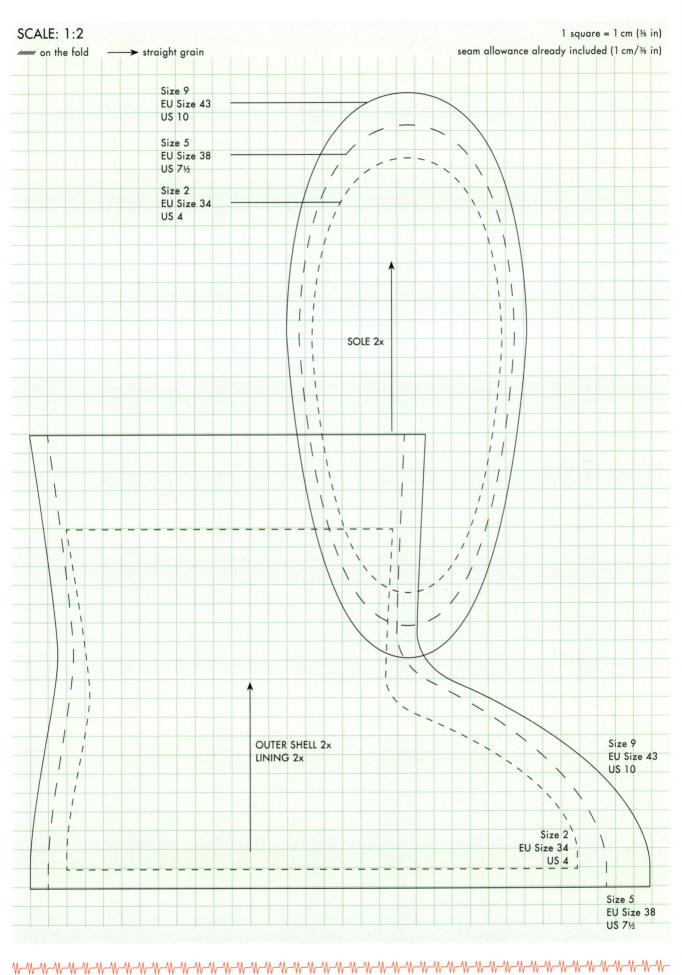

Size 9
EU Size 43
US 10

Size 5
EU Size 38
US 7½

Size 2
EU Size 34
US 4

SOLE 2x

OUTER SHELL 2x
LINING 2x

Size 9
EU Size 43
US 10

Size 2
EU Size 34
US 4

Size 5
EU Size 38
US 7½

1

Put your feet on a piece of paper and roughly trace the outline. Add 2 cm (¾ in) to the front and back of the pattern.

2

Double up the fabric for the outer shell, pin the pattern for the body to it and cut. Double up the fabric for the lining, pin the pattern for the body to it and cut. Pin the pattern for the soles to the lining fabric and cut out. Pin the patterns for the soles to the leather and cut out.

3

lining   outer shell

Pin the lining pieces right sides together and sew, leaving a 1-cm (⅜-in) seam allowance. Repeat with the outer shell pieces.

4

Pin the outer shell (inside out) to the leather sole. Pin the lining to the sole (right sides on the inside). Baste if necessary.

5

Sew each piece together, leaving a 1-cm (⅜-in) allowance.

6

Press under a 1-cm (⅜-in) hem for each piece, turn them right side out and slide the lining inside the outer shell.

Sew the hems of the bootie together.

Pin the elastic band roughly 6 cm (2⅜ in) up from the heel of the sole and sew both sides of the elastic band, gathering a bit of material in the back.

TIP: AS A FINISHING TOUCH, FOLD DOWN THE BOOT CUFF TO SHOW THE LINING FABRIC.

THE FAMILY HEADS CHRISTMAS BAUBLES

HERE IS A PROJECT THAT IS SURE TO BRING THE FAMILY TOGETHER. HANG THEM FROM A TREE. A GREAT WAY TO RECYCLE ODDS AND ENDS FROM PREVIOUS PROJECTS, THESE DECORATED BALLS WILL HAVE YOUR WHOLE FAMILY IN STITCHES DURING THE HOLIDAYS.

What you need:
- flesh-toned jersey, 20 x 10 cm (7⅞ x 4 in)
- different coloured fabrics or felt to decorate (hair, eyes, lips, moustaches, moles)
- stuffing (old stockings, cotton, hypoallergenic toy stuffing)
- nylon thread or fishing thread
- tapestry needle
- golden bead caps

1

Cut out a rectangle with the ratios of 2:1 in flesh-toned jersey. A nice size to start out with is a piece 20 x 10 cm (7⅞ x 4 in). Cut out a square for the hair and various pieces for the features.

2

Sew the features on the jersey fabric. This can be done on the machine or using embroidery stitches by hand. Different-coloured threads can also add to the design.

3

Turn the piece inside out, pin then sew the edges together, leaving a 5-mm (1/16-in) seam allowance.

4

Using nylon thread, work a line of running stitch regularly along the top edge of the head and pull tight to cinch. Tie a knot, but do not cut the thread.

5

Turn the piece right side out, passing the needle with the thread through the top hole. This will be used to hang your bauble.

6

Work a line of running stitch along the base.

7

Stuff your ball and then cinch the bottom. Knot the thread and cut.

8

Add a golden bead cap to the top thread for an elegant finish. Buttons can also be used to decorate the eyes. Use blush for cheeks.

SOFT FUZZY WOOL AND SOME
NEEDLES ARE ALL YOU NEED TO
GET ALL TIED UP IN KNITTING.

KNITTING ABBREVIATIONS

BO – bind off
CO – cast on
dec – decrease
inc – increase
k – knit
ktog – knit together
p – purl
St st – Stocking stitch
st(s) – stitch(es)

KNITTING

THE QUICK-KNIT FISHNET JUMPER

AN IDEAL PROJECT FOR THOSE SHORT ON TIME, THIS JUMPER CAN BE FINISHED IN ONE DAY. IT PLAYS HARD AND LOOSE WITH THE RULES, AND IS A GREAT BASIC FOR BEGINNERS. THE PATTERN CAN BE CHANGED AND ADAPTED BY ADDING DIFFERENT COLOURS AND WOOLS AT WILL. IMPERFECTIONS AND COLOUR CHOICE ONLY ADD TO ITS CHARM AND BEAUTY. SO GET KNITTING!

What you need for a medium-sized jumper:
– 20 mm (US 35) knitting needles
– 6 mm (US 10) knitting needles for the cuffs
– 3 to 4 x 50 g (2 oz) balls of knitting yarn in any colour and texture
– 1 x 50 g (2 oz) ball of knitting yarn for the cuffs (appropriate for 6 mm [US 10] needles)
– darning needle

FRONT: The body pieces are knitted from the bottom up. Using larger needles, CO 30 sts. Work St st for roughly 20 rows (depending on desired length of your jumper), starting with a knit row and ending with a purl row. Change the yarn at any time. Irregular changes will make this jumper more dynamic.

FINISHING THE NECKLINE: BO the middle 2 sts (fig 1). You have 28 sts, 14 on each side (fig 2). Finish each shoulder separately.

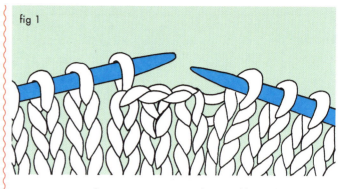
fig 1

SHOULDERS (front): Starting at the neckline, k2tog, k2tog, k10. Purl 1 row. K2tog, k2tog, k8. Purl 1 row (10 sts). Knit the next 4 rows in St st and dec (see p.84) 1 st at the neckline (6 sts). BO 6 sts. Repeat with the other shoulder (fig 3).

BACK: CO 30 sts. Work St st for at least 22 rows. End with a purl row. Like the front, you are knitting the jumper from the bottom up.

FINISHING THE BACK: After knitting almost to the top of the back (approximately 22 rows), BO the middle 4 sts (fig 1). You have 26 sts, 13 each side. Finish each shoulder separately (fig 2).

SHOULDERS (back): Starting at the neckline, k2tog, k2tog, k9. Purl 1 row. K2tog, k2tog, k7. Purl 1 row. K2tog, k2tog, k5. Purl 1 row and dec 1 st at the neckline. BO 6 sts. Repeat with the other shoulder (fig 3).

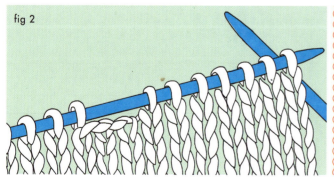
fig 2

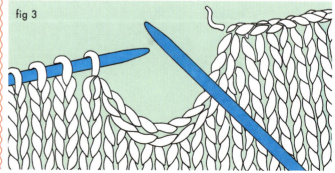
fig 3

THE QUICK-KNIT FISHNET JUMPER

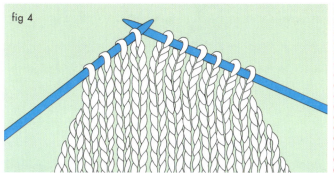

fig 4

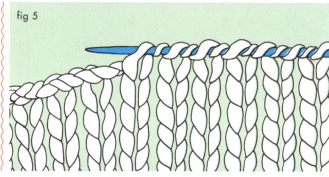

fig 5

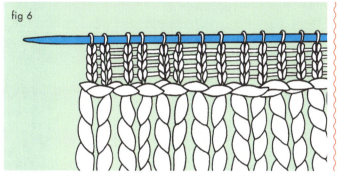

fig 6

fig 7

SLEEVES: The sleeves are knitted from the top down. CO 20 sts. Knit the first row and purl the second row. St st for the next 21 rows, dec at the beginning and end of every knit row. Repeat until you count 10 sts. St st the last 3 rows. Continue on to the cuffs. Repeat for the other sleeve (fig 4).

CUFFS: Change to smaller needles and yarn for ribbing the cuffs, neck and waistband. Pick up 10 sts. Inc in every second stitch of the first row (15 sts) (fig 5). Knit 4 rows with rib stitch. TIP: A classic rib stitch consists of alternating k2 and p2 until the end of the row. Remember that if you started with a knit stitch on one row, you should start with a purl stitch on the next. BO after 4 rows (fig 6).

NECKLINE: Change to smaller needles and yarn for ribbing the cuffs, neck and waistband. Pick up all the stitches in the neckline, inc in every second stitch of the first row. Work 4 rows in rib stitch (see cuffs) and BO (fig 6).

WAISTBAND: Change to smaller needles and yarn for ribbing the cuffs, neck and waistband. Pick up all the 30 stitches in the waist, inc in every second stitch of the first row (45 sts), and work in rib stitch to desired length (approx. 4 rows) and BO (fig 6).

FINISHING: Block the pieces and sew them together, using a darning needle (fig 7).

HOUSE SOCKS

COLD FEET? SOCK IT TO THEM! THIS IS AN EASY EVENING KNITTING PROJECT THAT USES UP ALL THOSE LEFTOVER ODDS AND ENDS IN YOUR YARN BAG. THE MISMATCHED COLOURS AND PATTERNS ARE PART OF THE CHARM OF THESE CUDDLY HOUSE SOCKS.

What you need:
One size fits all
– 4.5 mm (US 7) knitting needles
– 3 mm (US 2½) knitting needles
– 1 x 50 g (2 oz) ball of medium-weight yarn
– 1 x 100 g (4 oz) ball of bulky yarn

fig 1

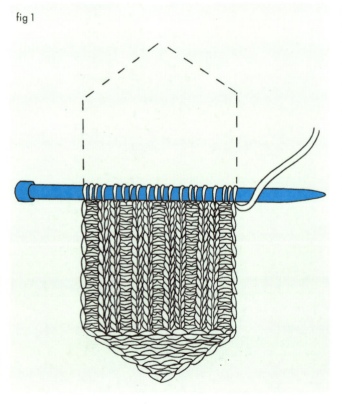

BASE:
Using smaller needles and medium-weight yarn, CO 2 sts.
ROW 1: Knit.
ROWS 2–20: Inc 1 st, knit to last st, inc 1 st. You have 40 sts.
ROW 21: Change to larger needles and bulky yarn. Work a ribbed stitch with a k2, p2 pattern until the body of the piece measures roughly 18–20 cm (7–8 in) (fig 1). Change to smaller needles and medium-weight yarn. Dec 1 st (see p. 84) at beginning and end of each row until you have 2 sts. BO the last stitch.

fig 2

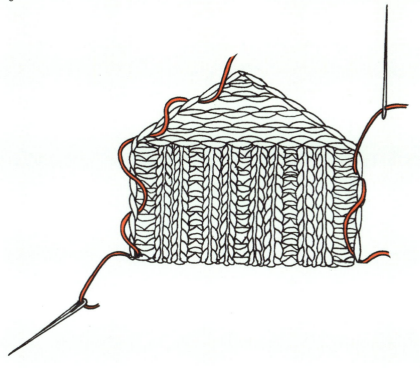

MAKING UP:
Fold the piece in half, right sides together. Whipstitch along all sides, except the side of the top triangle (fig 2).

THE KNITTED SNAKE

SNAKING UP YOUR WRIST OR AROUND YOUR NECK, POSING AS A SOFA SURPRISE, OR HIDING BEHIND A DOOR, THIS LITTLE KNIT PROJECT WILL SLINK QUICKLY OFF YOUR NEEDLES. PLAY AROUND WITH YARNS AND SIZES FOR ALL SORTS OF STRANGE AND WONDERFUL BEASTS.

What you need for a medium-sized scarf snake:
– 4.5 mm (US 7) knitting needles
– 50 g (2 oz) medium-weight black yarn
– 100 g (4 oz) bulky green yarn
– toy stuffing
– optional: flexible wire

INCREASE
To work additional stitches, use one of these methods:

fig 1

Use the right needle to pick up the loop just underneath the stitch and place it on the left needle. Knit a stitch from this loop and place it on the right needle.

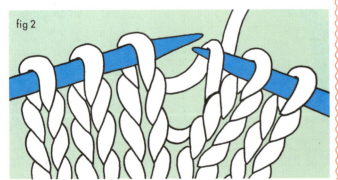

fig 2

Insert the right needle into the yarn between the stitches and place it on the left needle. Knit this new stitch.

DECREASE
To eliminate stitches, use one of these methods:

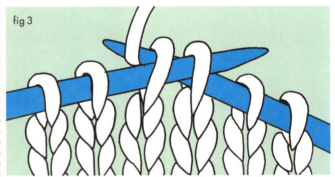

fig 3

Run the right needle through two stitches on your left needle and knit the two stitches together.

fig 4

Slip a stitch on the right needle, knit the next stitch, and move it to the right needle. Use your left needle to move the slipped stitch over the knitted stitch.

CO 9 sts with bulky yarn.
ROWS 1–6: St st.
ROWS 7–9: St st, inc 1 st in first 2 sts and last 2 sts.
You have 21 sts.
ROWS 10–18: St st.
ROW 19: St st, inc 1 st in first 2 sts and last 2 sts.
You have 25 sts.
ROW 20: Purl.
ROW 21: St st, inc 1 st in first 2 sts and last 2 sts.
You have 29 sts.
ROWS 22–32: St st.
ROWS 33–34: St st, dec 1 st in first 2 sts and last 2 sts.
You have 21 sts.
ROWS 35–43: With medium-weight yarn, St st.
ROWS 44–111: With bulky yarn, St st.
ROWS 112–113: With medium-weight yarn, St st.
ROWS 114–166: With bulky yarn, St st.
ROWS 167–175: St sts, dec in first and last st.
ROW 176: BO all sts.

ASSEMBLING THE SNAKE:
Press flat and fold the snake, right sides facing in, lengthways. Whipstitch the edges of the snake, from the head to the tummy. Repeat from the tail to the tummy leaving an opening of 15 cm (6 in) in the middle. Turn the snake inside out and stuff it with toy stuffing. Insert a flexible wire if using. Whipstitch the belly closed.

TIP: The wire helps hold the snake in shape.

SÉBASTIEN DAVIDTELEVISION'S JUMPER WITH A THEME

KNITTING A PICTURE CAN BE A USEFUL WAY TO DECORATE A JUMPER OR CREATE A KNITTED WALL TAPESTRY. SÉBASTIEN USES THESE TECHNIQUES TO MAKE HIS CELEBRATED DAVID BOWIE JUMPERS AND NOW YOU TOO CAN MAKE YOUR OWN ALBUM COVER JUMPER OR GIANT WALL HANGING. FIND YOURSELF A CHARITY SHOP ALBUM COVER THAT TICKLES YOUR FANCY AND TURN IT INTO A JUMPER. HAVE YOUR ART AND KNIT IT TOO.

Sébastien Davidtelevision is our very own 'knitting teacher in residence'. Every Tuesday evening Sébastien shows us all – complete amateurs and pros alike – the ABCs of knitting and how to realize your knitting dreams. When not sharing his knowledge with us, Séb collaborates regularly with French fashion house Balenciaga and makes his own knitwear designs. For all these reasons and more he was invited by Sweat Shop in spring 2010 to present his universe as our second 'Sweat Shop guest designer'. Influenced by electronic rock/wave music, Séb's jumper collection shows his own hand-knit take on vintage vinyl covers. He knits record sleeves on demand, with shapes and colours adapted to the buyer's wish. Every piece is unique – just how we love it.

un-garcon-octobre.blogspot.com

What you need:
- knitting needles
- yarn in any colour and texture

TIP: A perfect way to use any leftover yarn, changing the yarn can create different effects: use fluffy yarn for clouds, metallic yarn for cars and crepe yarn to make hair.

FAIR ISLE TECHNIQUE: This knitting technique is named after a tiny island off northern Scotland and is used to create multicoloured patterns. In this technique the inactive yarn is carried as a loose horizontal strand on the back of your piece while the active colour yarn is in use. When using this method, called 'stranding', don't leave the inactive colour at the back for more than five stitches. Long strands have a tendency to snag.

INTARSIA: Unlike the Fair Isle technique, the inactive yarn is simply left hanging in the back of your knitting and is carried vertically up to the next row when it is needed again. This allows you to create larger patterns and solid-coloured shapes and features. The hanging ends are woven into the back of the piece at the end.

For both techniques make sure to leave the hanging ends or loose strands in the back of your piece. A simple stocking stitch is advised, since complex stitch combinations distract from colour changes and patterns.

1 Start your knitting adventure by choosing an image or by making a sketch of your own.
2 Make a knitting sample to work out how many stitches a row will have and draw a grid of your knitting sample.
3 Trace outlines of the sketch or image on to the grid.
4 Colour the different features. Keep in mind that some of the details will be simplified.
5 Taking your coloured grid as a guide, start knitting the pattern from the bottom right of the grid.
Use the Fair Isle or intarsia technique depending on your design. Little details can be added at the end with embroidery.

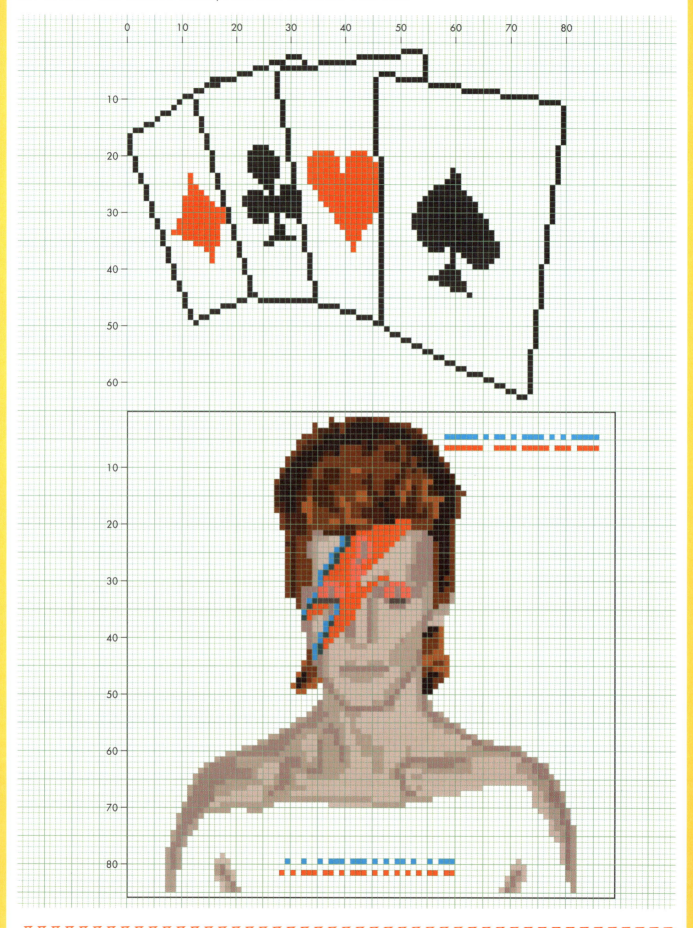

BALACLAVA

HOW BETTER TO PASS A RAINY WEEKEND THAN KNITTING A BALACLAVA? THE HYPNOTIC CLACKING OF THE NEEDLES IS THE SOUNDTRACK TO OUR AUTUMN EVES. IT IS AN ACT IN PREPARATION FOR THE COMING COLD, BEFORE WINTER'S ARRIVAL. THIS KNITTING PATTERN IS JUST THE BASIC SHAPE. YOU CAN CHANGE COLOURS OR ADD PATTERNS USING INTARSIA OR ANY OTHER ADVANCED KNITTING TECHNIQUE.

MOUSTACHE

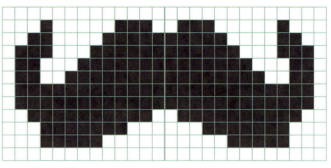

MOUTH

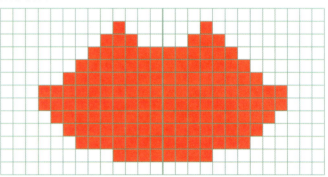

What you need:
– 3.5 mm (US 4) knitting needles
– 4 mm (US 6) knitting needles
– 4 x 50 g (2 oz) balls of yarn, in appropriate gauge (5 to 6 sts per inch):
2 x main colour
1 x contrasting colour 1
1 x contrasting colour 2

Using contrast colour and smaller needles, CO 72 sts.
ROW 1: K1, p1, repeat to end of row.
ROW 2: K1, p1, repeat to end of row.
These two rows form the rib. After the first two rows, change to main colour yarn.
Continue on in rib until the work measures 10 cm (4 in).

Change to larger needles.
Begin with a knit row and continue in garter stitch (knit every row) for 3.5 cm (1½ in).
NEXT ROW: K15, inc1, k14, inc1, k14, inc1, k14, inc1, knit to end. You have 76 sts.
Knit 3 rows.
NEXT ROW: K16, inc1, k15, inc1, k15, inc1, k15, inc1, knit to end. You have 80 sts.
Knit 3 rows.
NEXT ROW: K16, inc1, k16, inc1, k16, inc1, k16, inc1, knit to end. You have 84 sts.
Continue in garter stitch until the panel measures 6 cm (2½ in).

NEXT ROW, RIGHT SIDE: Start knitting in the mouth or moustache using the intarsia design in contrast colour, taking care that the design is knitted in the centre of the panel. The intarsia design is worked in stocking stitch.

Continue in garter stitch until the panel measures 13 cm (5 in) long.
NEXT ROW: Change to contrast yarn and knit.
NEXT ROW: K30, BO 24, k30.
NEXT ROW: K30, CO 24, k30.
NEXT ROW: Knit.
NEXT ROW: Change yarn back to main colour. Continue in garter stitch until the panel is 18 cm (7 in) long.

NEXT ROW: K12, k2tog, k12, k2tog, k12, k2tog, k12, k2tog, k12, k2tog, knit to end. You have 79 sts.
NEXT ROW: Knit.
NEXT ROW: K11, k2tog, k11, k2tog, k11, k2tog, k11, k2tog, k11, k2tog, knit to end. You have 74 sts.
NEXT ROW: Knit.
Reduce in the same way, every other row, until you are knitting 4 then knitting 2 together. Then decrease the same way on every row until 6 or 7 stitches are left. Break yarn and thread through remaining 7 stitches. Pull up tight and fasten off securely.

MAKING UP:
Sew the back seam with the main colour.

TIP: USING THE APPROPRIATE COLOURED YARN, WHIPSTITCH THE CENTRE OF THE EYE OPENING TO CREATE TWO SEPARATE EYE SOCKETS.

MADISON'S FINGER PUPPETS

THESE LITTLE PUPPETS CAN BE MADE IN A FLASH AND ARE AN IDEAL PRACTICE EXERCISE FOR BEGINNER KNITTERS. THE FINGER SIZE MAKES THEM A FAVOURITE WITH CHILDREN, AND THEY CAN BE CARRIED AROUND IN A HANDBAG. WE MADE FLASH GORDON AS AN EXAMPLE, BUT YOU CAN EASILY ADAPT THE PATTERN TO CREATE YOUR FAVOURITE SUPER-HERO OR FAIRY-TALE CHARACTER WITH A FEW CHANGES IN YARN COLOUR AND EMBROIDERY.

Madison O'Mara has creativity running in her blood. Born of a bohemian family that travels the world (her father is a photographer and her mother is a writer), knitting and crafting have always been second nature to her. As a little girl she made her own puppet theatre and, with her siblings, wrote and acted out plays. For her, knitting is not only a way to rid oneself of stress, it is a part of home that she carries around with her. A professional dancer by trade, she often goes to her auditions and rehearsals with her needles in hand. She loves Sweat Shop because it's a great place to get away from the hustle and bustle of life, and just work quietly. Our shy dreamer is always playing with yarn.

What you need to make 'Flash Gordon':
– 2.5–3 mm (US 1½–2½) knitting needles
– yarn in the appropriate gauge (6 to 8 sts per in) in white, light yellow, beige and a little bit of brighter yellow
– tapestry needle
– red and black thread

fig 1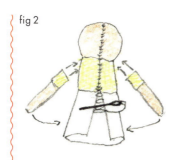
fig 2
fig 3
fig 4

BODY:
CO 21 sts with white yarn (fig1).
ROWS 1–4: K1, p1, repeat to end of row.
ROWS 5–12: St st.
ROWS 13–14: Change to light yellow yarn and knit to end of row. Purl 1 row.
ROW 15: K7, k2tog, k3, k2tog, k7. You have 19 sts.
ROW 16: Purl.
ROW 17: K7, k2tog, k1, k2tog, k7. You have 17 sts.
ROW 18: Purl.
ROW 19: Change to beige yarn. (K3, inc1) five times, k2. (Count 22 sts.)
ROWS 20–24: St st.
ROW 25: K2tog to the end of the row. You have 11 sts.
ROW 26: Purl.
ROW 27: K2tog five times, k1. BO 6 sts.

ARMS:
CO 5 sts with yellow.
ROWS 1–4: St st.
ROWS 5–11: Change to beige and work in St st.
ROW 12: P2tog, p1, p2tog.
Using a tapestry needle, pull thread through the remaining stitches and take off the knitting needle.
Sew the arms together down the side using whipstitch.

ASSEMBLY:
Sew the puppet together down the back, using whipstitch, and changing colours when necessary. Sew the arms to the body and the hands on the hip (fig2).

FINISHING:
Using a satin stitch, sew a band around the base of the shirt in thick red thread. Embroider an F on the shirt with satin stitch in red thread (fig3). Sew on bright yellow yarn for the hair, and sew the eyes, eyebrows and mouth in black thread (fig4).

ROCK OUT THE SECRET STORIES IN
YOUR CLOTHES AND SHOES WITH
THESE INSPIRATIONAL MAKEOVERS.

CUSTOMIZE

14　16　3/0　1/0　1　3　5　7　9

14　16　18　20　22　24　Ø0.6　Ø0.7

CROCHET CARDIGAN

DON'T THROW OUT NANNY'S DOILIES! A DELIGHTFULLY FEMININE WAY TO PERSONALIZE ANY JUMPER, THIS PROJECT RECYCLES OLD BITS OF LACE AS DECORATION, AND IT COVERS UP ANY STAINED OR MOTH-EATEN JERSEY.

What you need:
- cardigan
- lace or crocheted doily

1

Place your doily where you want (over the shoulder, on an elbow) and pin it flat to the cardigan. Baste the doily to the cardigan by hand.

2

Use a sewing machine to firmly stitch the doily in place.

3

Cut away the cardigan behind the doily to emphasize the lace effect.

4

Remove the basting stitches by hand.

MAKE YOUR OWN FABRIC

WHY SETTLE FOR ONE PATTERN
WHEN YOU WANT ALL FOUR?
INSPIRED BY THE ECLECTIC MIX OF
A FINE OLD ENGLISH LIVING ROOM,
THIS FABRIC CAN BE USED FOR
MORE THAN UPHOLSTERY. ITS
TEXTURES AND COLOURS BRIGHTEN
AND BEAUTIFY ANY GREY DAY.

What you need:
– 4 different fabrics

1

Pin the four fabrics together with
the sturdiest at the bottom and all
fabrics lying on the same grain.
Draw lines diagonal to the straight
grain from one corner to another.

2

Sew along the marked lines.

3

Cut between the lines through three
fabric layers, leaving the bottom
layer uncut.

HESTER'S PLAID-BLANKET CAPE

CAPES ARE DRAMATIC, FUNCTIONAL AND MYSTERIOUS. WHETHER YOU'RE SWANNING ABOUT DURING THE DAY OR SPENDING AN EVENING OUT WITH THE GIRLS, THIS SIMPLE CAPE IS SURE TO CATCH EVERYONE'S EYE. DO AS HESTER DOES AND MAKE THOSE OLD BLANKETS MORE THAN JUST SOFA ORNAMENTS. YOU'LL FEEL LIKE A WOODLAND LASS OR A LADY FROM THE MOORS.

Hester Velthuis hails from the small Dutch town of Geldrop, already famous for producing Viktor Horsting of Viktor and Rolf. Her elfish presence hides a brilliant mind that is as much drawn to psychiatry as it is to fashion. 'Clothes say more than people think. Children wear amazing clothes because they combine colours in ways most people don't think of.' As a little girl she would wear only trouser suits in matching patterns, and her approach remains eccentric and child-like. Inspired by fabric, she plays with drape and form in her designs, creating whimsy from something as banal as a blanket. She brings a twinkling spirit to Sweat Shop, which she says reminds her of home.

What you need for a medium-sized knee-length cape:
- any plaid blanket, about 140 x 280 cm (55 x 110 in)
- cord, 10 cm (4 in)
- button, about 3 cm (1¼ in) diameter

TIP: Any thick fabric will work if you don't have a blanket; use thinner fabric for a summer cape.

www.hestervelthuis.com

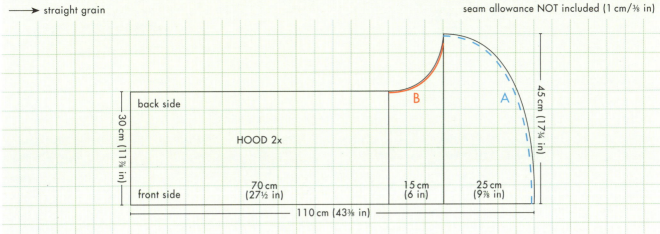

→ straight grain

1 square = 5 cm (2in)
seam allowance NOT included (1 cm/⅜ in)

back side

30 cm (11⅞ in)

HOOD 2x

B

A

45 cm (17¾ in)

front side

70 cm (27½ in)

15 cm (6 in)

25 cm (9⅞ in)

110 cm (43⅜ in)

1

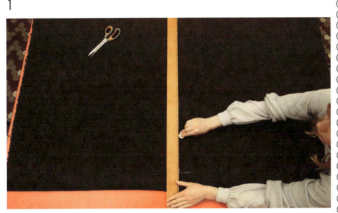

Measure and cut a main piece of fabric 180 x 140 cm (71 x 55 in). Fold the fabric in two crossways (so you have a folded piece measuring 90 x 140 cm (35 x 55 in), right sides facing in. Draw a line down the centre of the fabric, at right angles to the fold.

2

Measure 7 cm (2¾ in) down from the fold and draw a half-circle about 20 cm (7⅞ in) in diameter.

3

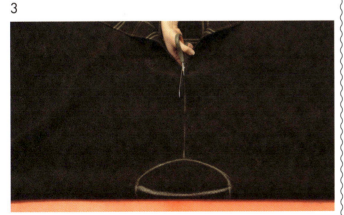

Draw a shallower curve on the other side of the half-circle to create the back neckline. Cut the top layer of fabric along the centre line as far as the circle, then cut out the circle.

4

Fold the leftover fabric from Step 1 in two lengthways and pin the pattern on to it. Trace the pattern on to the fabric, adding a 1-cm (⅜-in) seam allowance and cut the shape out. You now have two separate pieces for the hood.

5

Pin the round edge (A) of both pieces together, right sides together.

6

Sew along the rounded edge, allowing for a 1-cm (⅜-in) seam allowance.

7

Unfold the hood and pin the curve (B) to the back neckline of the main piece, right sides together.

8

Sew the pieces together, allowing for a 1-cm (⅜-in) seam allowance.

9

Cut pockets to your desired size out of the remaining fabric. (Hester used two 22 x 18 cm/8⅝ x 7 in pieces.)

10

Pin the pockets evenly on each side of the front of the cape at the desired height. Sew the pockets on three sides to the main piece, leaving the top open, allowing for a 1-cm (⅜-in) seam allowance.

11

Cut a piece of cord to form a loop large enough to allow the button to pass through with a bit of extra allowance.

12

Attach the loop 4 cm (1½ in) under the hood by covering the end with a little square of fabric and stitching along the edges and diagonally across the square in both directions.

13

Sew the button opposite the loop.

TIP: This cape has been designed to have no hem, but feel free to add a hem if you prefer.

SLEEPING MASK

SLEEPING BEAUTY, WHERE ART THOU?
SLEEPING MASKS, THE PERFECT
PARTNER TO YOUR PRECIOUS
REJUVENATING SLEEP, ARE OFTEN
TOSSED UNDER THE BED OR INTO
A SIDE DRAWER. THAT WON'T
HAPPEN ONCE YOU'VE DONE THIS
PROJECT. JUST A PINCH OF FAIRY-TALE
DELIGHT MAKES THE PERFECT
SUNGLASSES FOR YOUR DREAMS.

1

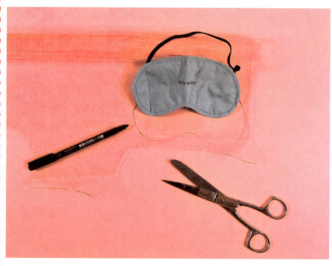

Trace the outline of the sleeping mask on to the plastic film. Cut out the plastic film.

What you need:
- sleeping mask
- an old fairy-tale book
- plastic film

- sticky tape or glue
- pen

2

Trace the outline of the plastic film on to an image from the vintage fairy-tale book. Cut out.
TIP: Use glue or tape to make a collage from the images and then cut out the mask shape.

3

Pin the plastic film to the image and stitch along 3 mm (⅛ in) from the edge.

4

Stitch the image-covered plastic film to the original sleeping mask along the previously stitched edge.

CUSTOMIZE YOUR OLD SHOES

YOU KNOW WHAT IT'S LIKE:
YOU FIND THE PERFECTLY CUT SHOE
AND IT HAS ONE ODD BLEMISH
OR IT'S THE WRONG COLOUR.
WELL, BULLY FOR THE SHOE!
LET YOUR INNER GRAFFITI ARTIST
OUT TO PLAY AND GET THOSE
PUMPS GUSSIED UP. AFTER ALL,
YOU ARE AN URBAN PRINCESS.

What you need:
- leather shoes
- leather spray paint
- lace or wool
- masking tape
- old newspapers

1

Using masking tape, cover up anything you do not want painted, including graphic lines, flower shapes, letters, dots or stars as desired. Attach lace to create a pattern or use other shapes for decorative relief.

2

Your shoes are now ready to be sprayed. Spray in a ventilated area on newspapers. Allow the shoes to dry for one hour.

Remove the masking tape, lace or other shapes.

TIP: THE SAME PROCESS CAN BE DONE ON VIRTUALLY ANY LEATHER FABRIC. YOUR HANDBAGS, SKIRTS AND PURSES ARE PROBABLY ALREADY LOOKING ON IN ENVY.

VA-VA-VOOM JACKET

THE MOTORCYCLE JACKET, A PERENNIAL URBAN CLASSIC, IS GIVEN A ROMANTIC MAKEOVER BY UNDERGROUND FRENCH GODDESS VAVA DUDU. LONG WORN BY SEXY GIRLS FOR AN EDGY LOOK, THE MOTORCYCLE JACKET WAS TAKEN OVER BY PUNK ROCK IN THE '70S, AND IT'S ONE WARDROBE PIECE THAT IS NO STRANGER TO EMBELLISHMENT. IN THIS PROJECT WE TAKE A FEW ODDS AND ENDS, BEADS AND THREAD, AND SHOW YOU HOW A LITTLE LOVE CAN GO A LONG WAY. EVEN GAGA WOULD BE AGOG.

Vava Dudu is beyond cool. Her legendary style, personality, clothes and music would make Warhol green with envy. For her *le freak, c'est chic.* But who is this fabulous creature of the night, with her mutant multiheaded jackets, her surreal polyester shifts and her Miro-meets-Daniel Johnston drawings? Well, to be tawdry, one could call her a stylist. Björk and Lady Gaga have both been styled by her and dressed in her clothes. Her pieces are like chimeras: serpentine sexual appeal, regally lioness form, offbeat goat-like sense of humour. One could say Vava Dudu is a modern Parisian goddess: she rules its nightlife and epitomizes the radical spirit of its street fashion. One could also say she is a dear friend: Sissi and Vava have been friends for years. But frankly, we just like Vava because of the way she is: incomparable.

vavadudu.blogspot.com

What you need:
- vintage motorcycle jacket
- beads
- card
- thick thread
- drawing paper
- plain cotton fabric
- waterproof marker
- safety pins

TIP: Anything you feel can be attached to your jacket is fine.

1

Draw your design on a grid in preparation for bead weaving. Each coloured-in square on the grid corresponds to one bead.

2

Make little cuts in each end of the card corresponding to the number of lines in the grid.

3

Number each line on the grid.

4

Wrap thread around the piece of card for each line.

5

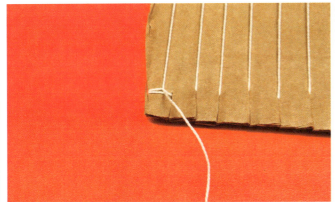

Make sure there is firm tension in each line of thread, then tie the ends off with a knot.

6

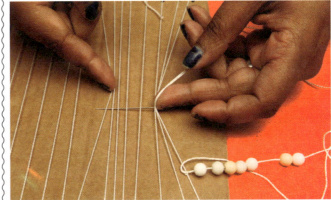

Using needle and thread, tie the end of your thread to the start of the grid for the first row. Looking at the design for the first row, thread on the corresponding coloured bead for each square on the grid.

7

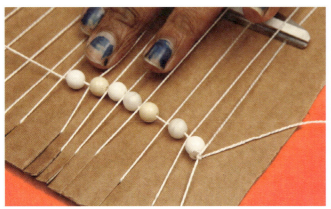

Place the beads so that they each lie in their own column, keeping the thread with the beads under the thread of the grid.

8

Keeping the thread fairly taut, bring the needle from under the grid and thread it back through the beads. Your thread should run above the grid thread.

9

Repeat for each row, threading the beads, placing them under the grid thread and then threading the needle back through them above the grid until the design is finished.

10

Knot the work after the last bead to keep it together.

11

This is an example of how we made a word with beads.

12

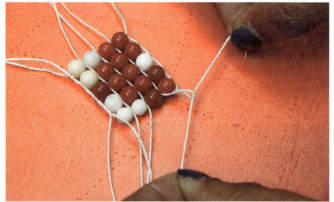

Cut the beadwork from the card support. Tie off all of the ends, two by two, to keep the beads from slipping out.

13

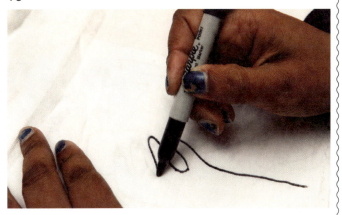

Place your drawing under a piece of thin cotton. Using a waterproof marker, copy the drawing on to the fabric.

14

Cut the drawing out. Place the beaded work and the drawing on the jacket, and either stitch them directly on to the leather, or simply attach them with safety pins for that punk-rock attitude.

DECORATE YOUR WORLD WITH
WHIMSY. FOR JOY, FOR FUN,
WITH LOVE.

DECORATION

BONBON, DRAUGHT BEGONE!

THIS BEAUTIFUL BONBON DRAUGHT
EXCLUDER IN PLAID AND VINYL IS
NOT ONLY EFFICIENT AT WARDING
OFF WINTER CHILLS, ITS GRAPHIC
COLOURS ALSO ADD A DESIGN
ELEMENT TO ANY ROOM.

What you need:
- resistant fabric,
  150 x 50 cm (59 x 20 in),
  perhaps an old plaid
  blanket

- strong fabric to
  decorate (we used
  vinyl)
- strong, pretty cord

- filling (stockings,
  cotton, old clothes)
- teflon foot on sewing
  machine (if using vinyl
  fabric)

- tapestry needle

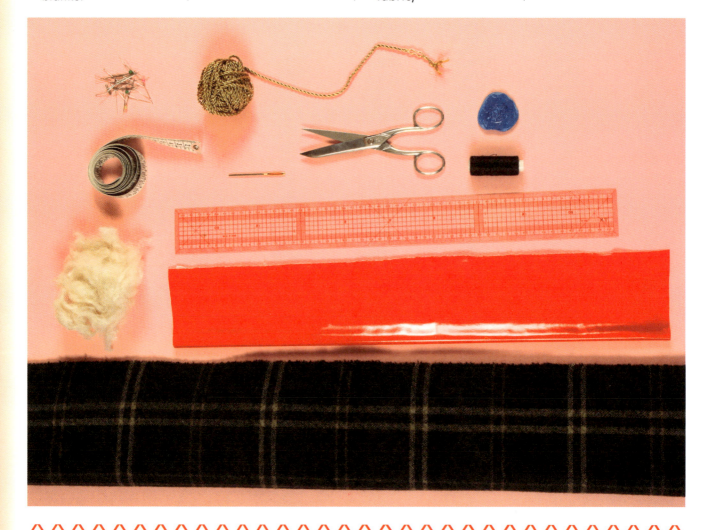

1

Measure the width of your door. Cut a piece of fabric to this measurement and 50 cm (20 in) wide. The width can be changed to make your bonbon fatter or thinner.

2

For the ties on each side, cut the fabric of your choice to the same width as the main piece. The length should be roughly half that of the main piece.

3

Place the tie on the edge of your main piece, right sides together; pin and stitch, leaving a 1-cm (⅜-in) seam allowance. Repeat on the other side.

4

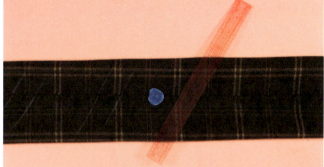

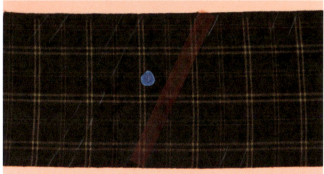

Decorate your bonbon. In our example we made vinyl stripes that go around the main piece. Using a ruler and a protractor, cut out stripes that are the appropriate length to cover the bonbon diagonally.

6

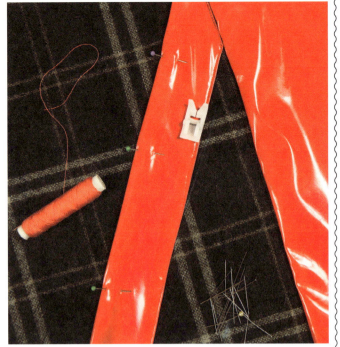

For whatever width of stripe you decide, add 2 cm (¾ in). Fold under 1 cm (⅝ in) on each side of each stripe and pin on to the main piece. Sew with a 2 mm (scant) edge stitch on both sides of the strip. TIP: vinyl fabric sews easily with a teflon foot.

7

Stuff the stripes. Use a wooden dowel, knitting needle or even the long handle of a wooden spoon to help get the stuffing in.

8

Fold the whole piece in half widthways, right sides together, and stitch, allowing for a 1-cm (⅜-in) seam allowance.

9

Turn the tube inside out and fold in the edges of the two end ties.

Pass a running stitch of cord along the right side of the bonbon, also taking in the folded-in edges of the ties.

Pull the cord tightly to cinch, then knot. Leave a long end on the cord that you can then use to attach to a doorknob or hook. Stuff your bonbon. Pass a running stitch with another piece of cord along the left side of the bonbon, again taking in the folded-in edges of the ties. Cinch, knot and leave enough length to attach to a doorknob or hook.

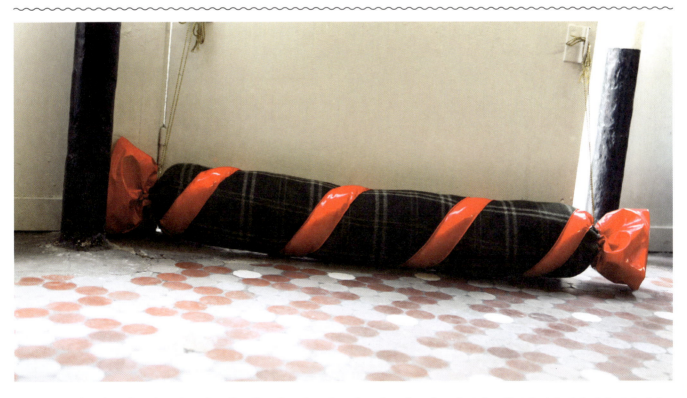

DELPHINE'S JEANS MASK

HERE AT SWEAT SHOP WE BELIEVE THAT IMPERFECTION AND DIFFERENCE SHOULD BE EMBRACED AND CELEBRATED. DELPHINE'S PROJECT IS FOR THOSE WHO SEW A LITTLE ON THE WILD SIDE. THIS MASK IS ALL ABOUT MISTAKES: SHOWING ONE'S STITCHES, CUTTING ON THE FLY, PLAYING WITH CONTRASTS AND TEXTURE. IT TAKES THOSE PAIRS OF UNWEARABLE DESTROYED JEANS AND RECYCLES THEM INTO GORGEOUS MAD MASKS. THE INSTRUCTIONS ARE JUST A STARTING POINT. LET YOUR IMAGINATION LOOSE AND YOU WILL NEVER LOOK AT YOUR JEANS THE SAME WAY AGAIN.

Delphine Mille knows there is magic in make-believe. A self-professed amateur, Delphine uses the virtue of her inability to sew to let chance work its charm. Though she makes her living teaching applied arts in Lyon, her strong belief in collective practice brought her to Sweat Shop's doors. We've unmasked our resident Art Brut practitioner and find her works to be a cipher for all that is powerful about the process of making.

What you need:
- old jeans
- strong thread
- jeans needle for the sewing machine
- foam rubber (buy it or take a snap-off knife to that ugly old mattress)
- oval pattern about 30 x 40 cm (12 x 16 in)

delphine1000.blogspot.com

1

For the main front and back pieces, cut off the legs of a pair of jeans. Cut off 10 cm (4 in) from the bottom hem of the legs. Cut each piece in half lengthways.

2

Place the prepared pattern on the wrong side of the material from step 1, and add 3 cm (1¼ in) around the edges. Cut out and repeat for the second piece.

3

If you are using your mask as a wall ornament, simply add a cord by gluing it with two round fabric pieces.

4

VARIATION: If you choose to make a rucksack, you can use the waistband for the straps. Sew both ends to the back piece, with the button facing out.

5

For the face have some fun. Delphine used the hem left over from step 1 for the mouth. She made little cuts regularly all around the edge, about 2 cm (¾ in) deep. Place the mouth at the desired spot and fix it by first gluing and then stitching it on. You can make the mouth smaller by reducing the circumference of the leg fabric.

6

For the nose, trace and cut the crotch of the jeans along the back seam towards the waistband, keeping some of the leg seam.

7

Fold the piece into a loop to form the nose, fix it (with glue or pins) and stitch.

8

For the eyes fold a piece of fabric in two, cut out a circle and cut the circle down the middle.

9

Use part of the hem from the leg for eyelids. Attach all the pieces to create the eyes, then use a seam ripper to fray the material for the lashes.

10

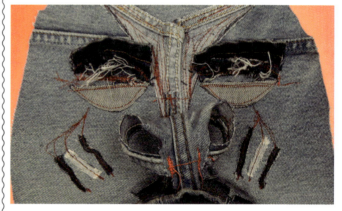

For the little but no-less important details such as scars, Delphine simply cuts out strips and sews them on. You can use cloth paint or other materials. And remember: mistakes are part of the charm.

11

Cut out the pocket for the forehead, leaving 3 cm (1¼ in) on the top. Pin it to the face of your mask, wrong sides together, and sew it on.

12

Using your pattern and a snap-off knife, cut out the foam rubber.

13

Measure the circumference and depth of your foam. Cut out a piece of jeans with those dimensions, adding 3 cm (1¼ in) to each side and a 1-cm (⅜-in) seam allowance to the length.

14

Pin the strip all around the face of the mask, wrong sides together. The stitches are meant to be visible. Stitch, allowing for a 3-cm (1¼-in) seam allowance, lifting the mask from time to time, going around and adjusting the circumference if necessary. Stitch the strip ends together.

15

Now pin the pocket to the face and stitch it on.

16

Place the foam inside the face. Pin then stitch the back on, leaving a 3-cm (1¼-in) seam allowance. If making a bag, attach a zip at the top of the back piece.

17

Attack the piece with a seam ripper or scissors for any finishing or fraying touches.

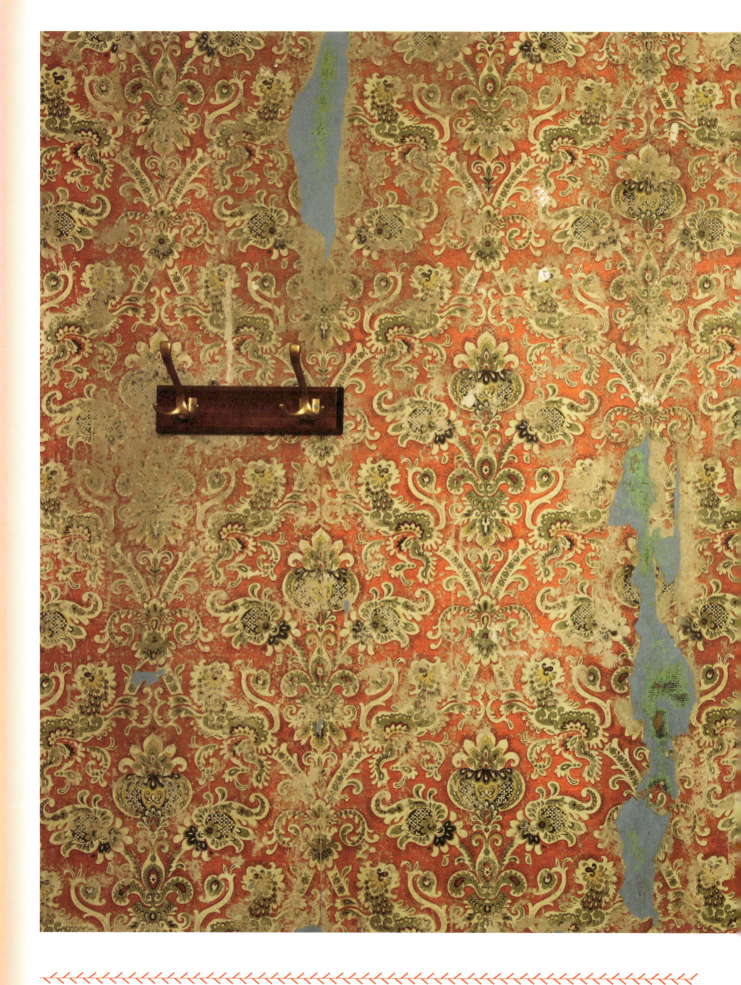

Delphine's Jeans Mask & Tanker's Vintage Wall

TANKER'S VINTAGE WALL

Momo Ayada, Pepijn and Floris van Looy are Tanker, a team of art directors. However, to be truthful, their real job is creative problem solving. If you were to throw them on the moon and ask them to re-create a living room, they would do just that and probably build you a spaceship to boot. Masters at their craft, they have whipped up sets and props for feature films, shorts, commercials and music videos, working with materials to hand. Every inch of Sweat Shop, from floor to ceiling, was designed by these Belgian whizz-kids. Sweat Shop's trademark spirit and aesthetic would not have been possible without them.

Self-described risk takers, Tanker searches for solutions outside the box. Arriving in the desert in the sultanate of Oman, they found themselves confronted with the astounding task of creating complicated sets with a very limited budget. After a quick dash to the sea, where they dunked their heads in the water, they came up with solutions for the whole project. A couple of sand-filled days later, people were skiing on the dunes.

So, the next time you need to make a world, build a tree to climb or plant a garden of earthly delights, just remember that Tanker is there. Sweat Shop's superheroes are always looking for a challenge.

www.tanker.be

THE WALL AT THE BACK OF SWEAT SHOP FEATURES A GORGEOUS VINTAGE WALLPAPER FACADE. THE AGEING METHOD INVOLVES A VERY SIMPLE PROCESS OF LAYERING PAINT AND WALLPAPER, THEN SANDING IT OFF.

What you need to paint the wall:
– wall paint of various different colours
– rollers, brushes

1

Use a roller to paint your first layer. Start with a light base colour. Paint four layers of different colours, leaving the paint to dry completely after each layer.

TIP: Before you start ensure the wall is clean and dry. However, cracks and bumps should be left on – they will add to the vintage feel of the wall.

What you need to wallpaper the wall:
- wallpaper table or any good working surface
- vintage wallpaper
- folding ruler
- scissors
- cup of water
- scraping tool or smoothing brush
- wallpaper paste

2

Apply wallpaper using glue and scraping tools, making sure your patterns line up.

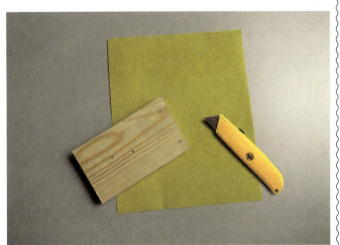

What you need to destroy the surface:
- sandpaper
- sanding block
- snap-off knife

3

Once the wallpaper is dry, you can begin the ageing process. Distress it in areas by rubbing with sandpaper. Trim off the surplus with a snap-off knife.

EMILY'S FLOWERPOT COSY

MAKING YOUR OWN YARN WITH OLD PIECES OF CLOTHING IS NOT ONLY EASY AND ECONOMICAL, IT'S A RIOT OF COLOUR. A PUCKISH TAKE ON THE RAG RUG, THE YARN CAN THEN BE USED TO KNIT ALL SORTS OF OBJECTS. IN THIS CASE WE USED IT TO KNIT A COSY FOR A FLOWER-POT. ONCE THE YARN IS MADE, THIS PROJECT CAN BE KNITTED IN LESS THAN ONE DAY.

Emily Towers is deeply interested in the environmental impact of the fashion industry. In an age where trends pass by in a flash of months, she believes the destructive effects of consumerism can be counteracted by daily choices: recycling clothing and creating communities to make and trade clothing and ideas. It is this passion that brought her not only to a master's at Central Saint-Martin's, but also to Sweat Shop, where we share that idealism. Coming from a deep family tradition of tailoring and knitting, Emily has always been making and designing clothes – not just for fashion, but for life. emilytowers.co.uk

What you need:
– in this example we used a flowerpot that was 220 cm (86½ in) in circumference and 21 cm (8¼ in) in depth
– 4 vintage men's shirts; you can use any old garment in thin cotton or lightweight jersey
– 10 mm (US 15) knitting needles

fig 1

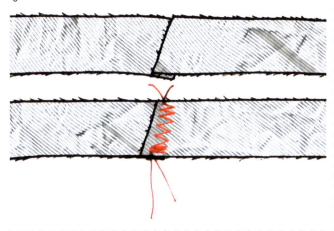

fig 2

fig 3

fig 4

1 Cut strips from the backs and arms of the shirts, 2 cm (¾ in) wide. TIP: If you are using fabric shirts, cut along the bias to reduce fraying. If you are using jersey, cut the strips along the stretch grain (fig 1).

2 Sew the strips end to end to form one long strip. This is your yarn for the project (fig 2). TIP: Don't forget to mix colours and patterns.

3 For a pot of the size we used, cast on 38 stitches (fig 3).

4 Knit in stocking stitch until the knitted panel wraps around the circumference of the pot (fig 4). Bind off.

5 Using whipstitch, join the panel's ends.

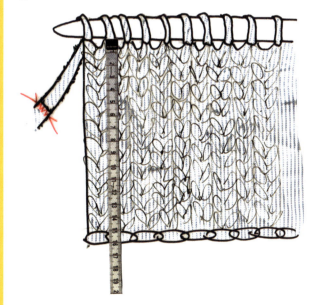

ALL THOSE LITTLE TIPS AND TRICKS
TO HELP ADD A FINISHING TOUCH
TO ANY DESIGN.

A BALLSY PROJECT

EVERYONE NEEDS MORE BALLS. AT WORK, TO GIVE AS A PRESENT, AS A HOLIDAY ORNAMENT, FOR SPORT OR JUST TO KICK AROUND, THESE BALLS TAKE NO TIME TO WHIP UP. STUFF THEM WITH SOME CATNIP FOR A FABULOUS KITTY PRESENT. MAKE THEM BIGGER OR SMALLER, HOWEVER YOU LIKE IT. A NEW BALL IS RIGHT AT YOUR FINGERTIPS.

1 Choose one of the available shapes and cut the pattern to size on a piece of paper or card.
2 Place the pattern on your fabric and cut out the number of pieces indicated for each shape.
3 Stitch or sew every edge, right sides facing in, for each piece, leaving a small opening.
4 Turn the fabric inside out and stuff.
5 Finish the final seam by hand.

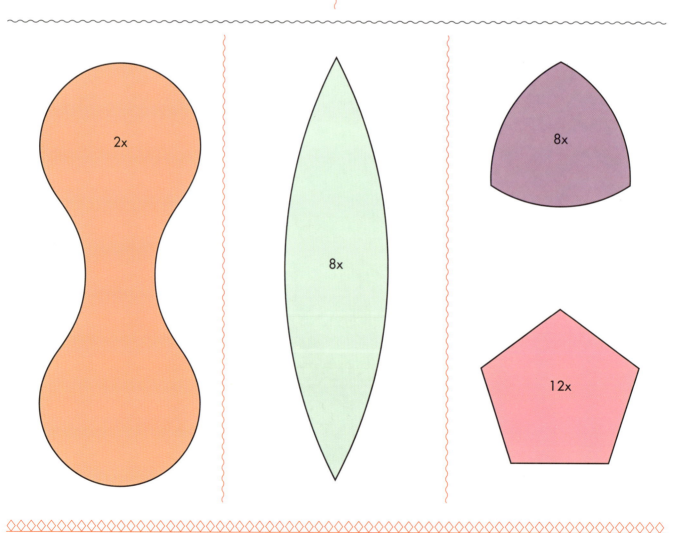

WEAVING LEATHER

1 Use a ruler to draw lines on the back of your main leather piece (fig 1).
   TIP: How you draw your lines affects how your piece looks. Play with asymmetry and chance.
2 Use a seam ripper to prick along the lines.
3 Cut separate strips of leather and weave them in tightly, one after another (fig 2).

NOT JUST FOR CAVEMEN OR COWBOYS, LEATHER IS ONE OF THOSE NOBLE MATERIALS THAT AGES GRACEFULLY. AND, WHILE EVERYONE HAS SEEN WOVEN LEATHER, FEW PEOPLE ACTUALLY KNOW HOW EASY IT IS TO MAKE. ONE OF THE MOST BASIC LEATHERCRAFT TECHNIQUES, IT CAN BE SEEN TODAY IN EVERYTHING FROM HANDBAGS TO INLAYS IN SHOES. WEAVING ADDS GREAT TEXTURE AND CONTRAST TO LEATHER, ADDING TO ITS ENDURING APPEAL.

fig 1

fig 2

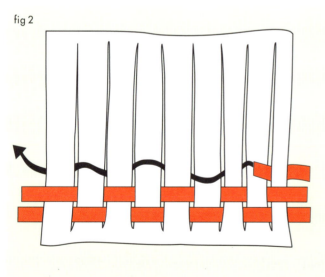

THE MAGIC PLAIT

THIS PLAITING TECHNIQUE IS A GREAT STARTING POINT FOR BAGS, BELTS OR BRACELETS. IT WORKS PARTICULARLY WELL WITH LEATHER AND IS AS MYSTERIOUS AS THE MÖBIUS STRIP. THE MAGIC PLAIT IS REMARKABLY EASY TO UNDERSTAND ONCE YOU GET YOUR HANDS ON IT. PLAITS ARE BETTER, BABY.

1 Cut two parallel lines into your piece to get three equal-sized strips (fig 1).
2 Place the red strip over the green strip. Place the brown strip over the centre strip, now red (fig 2).
3 Pass the bottom end between the brown and green strips, front to back (fig 3).
4 Untwist the bottom end to the right in order to have both ends on the front side (fig 4).
5 Pass the bottom end between green and brown, front to back (fig 5).
6 Repeat to finish the braid (fig 6).

fig 1

fig 2
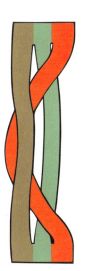

fig 3
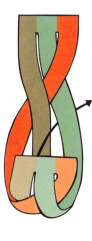

fig 4

fig 5

fig 6

LOOP KNITTING

LEARN HOW TO KNIT LONG AND DANGLING LOOPS TO ADD A SOFT AND WARM TEXTURE TO YOUR KNITTING. THICK YARN WILL GIVE A PADDED EFFECT, ESPECIALLY IF KNITTED ON EVERY STITCH, WHILE THINNER YARN WILL YIELD A MORE TEXTURAL EFFECT. IT TAKES A BIT OF FIDDLING, BUT ONCE UNDER YOUR THUMB, THIS TECHNIQUE GIVES YOUR JACKET, JUMPER, PILLOW, TEA COSY OR BLANKET A GREAT SHAGGY LOOK. WORK WITH THICK UNBLEACHED WOOL FOR A NORDIC-STYLE RUG. THERE ARE MANY DIFFERENT WAYS TO CREATE LOOPS. THIS ONE WILL MAKE A LOOP ON THE BACK OF YOUR WORK.

1 Working on a knit row, knit to the stitch where you want your loop to start.
2 Twist the yarn twice around your left forefinger.
3 Knit the next stitch by pulling both loops of yarn from the left forefinger through the stitch (fig 1), but do not slip the stitch from the left-hand needle and do not release the loop from the left forefinger.
4 Knit the same stitch again through the back loop (fig 2) and slip it onto the right needle.
5 Release the loop from the forefinger. At this point you can adjust the length of your loop. You now have three stitches on the right needle. Slip the first two stitches you made over the third to fix the loop (fig 3).

fig 1

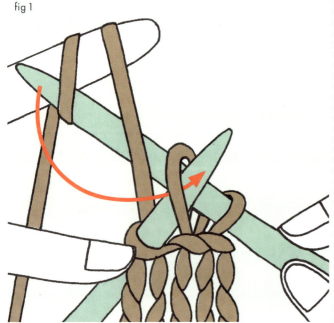

fig 2

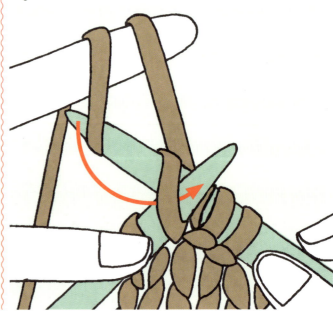

fig 3

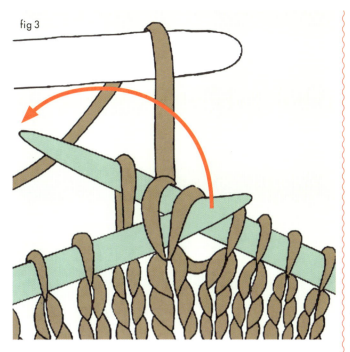

TIP 1: Leave your loops intact or cut them for a plush effect. You do not have to make a loop in every stitch – vary for volume.

TIP 2: Use polyester yarn with a rough finish if you want to make a flannel. The loop technique will help facilitate exfoliation.

THREADS: A PHOTO LOVE STORY

Directed by Lia R. Pàris
Photography: Mélanie Petitqueux
Actresses: Martena Duss,
Sissi Holleis, Isabell Thrun,
Audrey Bee, Marie Finot,
Lia R. Pàris

www.thisisvasistas.com

RECIPES

EVERYBODY LIKES CAKE. THOSE QUIET AFTERNOONS WITH THE HUM OF KNITTING AND SEWING IN THE BACKGROUND WOULDN'T BE COMPLETE WITHOUT A LITTLE BREAK. PART OF THE SWEAT SHOP LIFE IS BRINGING BACK ALL THAT FRESH-BAKED GOODNESS. THE GENTLE PERFUMES OF SUGAR AND SPICE ARE WHAT MAKE A HOME SO NICE. MOST OF THESE RECIPES HAVE COME VIA OUR FAMILIES, OUR SWISS AND AUSTRIAN HERITAGE, AND ARE PART OF OUR HISTORY. FROM HEAVENLY FRANGIPANE TO SPICED NORDIC CAKES, WE HOPE YOU ENJOY OUR SMALL TASTE OF THE SWEET LIFE.

SISSI'S CHOCOLATE CAKE 140

MARTENA'S ALMOND–CHOCOLATE CAKE 141

*MATCHA CHOCOLATE COOKIES FROM BOB'S JUICE BAR 142

GÉNOISE À LA FRAISE 144

HOME-MADE SYRUP 145

NORDIC CARDAMOM BREAD 146

EPISTLE TO A FRIEND 147

SWEAT SHOP TOP 30 148

*Masterclass sections are indicated in yellow throughout the book. These are special tutorials given by professionals who are regular collaborators with Sweat Shop.

SISSI'S CHOCOLATE CAKE

PREPARATION TIME: 25 min / BAKING TIME: 25 min

What you need:
- 200 g (7 oz) baking chocolate (or any good-quality plain chocolate)
- 5 eggs
- 250 g (9 oz) butter (softened)
- 200 g (7 oz) caster sugar
- 2 tbsp cocoa powder
- 200 g (7 oz) ground almonds
- icing sugar (for dusting)

COUNT YOUR LUCKY STARS BECAUSE THIS CLASSIC CHOCOLATE CAKE IS SISSI'S SPECIALTY. PASSED THROUGH GENERATIONS AND MADE WITHOUT FLOUR, ITS RICHNESS AND INTENSITY ARE LIKE A HAIKU TO THE PURE ELEGANCE OF CHOCOLATE. IRRESISTIBLE.

Preparation:
1 Preheat your oven to 180°C (350°F/gas mark 4).
2 Break the chocolate into a heat-proof bowl and set over a saucepan of barely simmering water (don't let the bottom of the bowl touch the water) until melted.
3 Separate the eggs and beat the egg whites until stiff.
4 Beat the butter, egg yolks and granulated sugar together until fluffy.
5 Add the melted chocolate and cocoa.
6 Fold in the egg whites and ground almonds.
7 Bake in a buttered 20-cm (8-in) round fluted cake tin for 25 min.
8 Turn the cake out and leave it to cool, then dust with icing sugar.
TIP: Use a plastic or paper doily as a pattern on which to dust the confectioners' sugar.

MARTENA'S ALMOND–CHOCOLATE CAKE

PREPARATION TIME: 25 min / BAKING TIME: 45 min

What you need:
- 4 eggs
- 200 g (7 oz) caster sugar
- a pinch of salt
- 1 tbsp vanilla sugar
- 250 ml (9 fl oz) single cream
- 100 g (3½ oz) plain chocolate
- 250 g (9 oz) ground almonds (or any other kind of ground nut)
- icing sugar (for dusting)

THIS IMPOSSIBLY FLUFFY FRANGIPANE CAKE STUFFED WITH GOOEY CHOCOLATE BITS IS ONE OF SWEAT SHOP'S GREATEST HITS. THE LIGHTNESS OF THIS CAKE BELIES ITS DECADENCE. WE LOVE ALMONDS, BUT YOU CAN MAKE THIS WITH ALMOST ANY KIND OF GROUND NUT. EASY TO MAKE, WE HOPE THIS LITTLE TASTE OF LUXURY BECOMES A REGULAR IN YOUR KITCHEN.

Preparation:

1 Preheat your oven to 180°C (350°F/gas mark 4).
2 Separate the eggs.
3 Whisk the egg whites until stiff.
4 Beat the egg yolks with the sugar until fluffy.
5 Whisk the salt, vanilla sugar and cream into the egg yolk mixture.
6 Break the chocolate into chunks and stir in with the egg yolk, vanilla sugar and cream mixture.
7 Add the ground nuts.
8 Fold in the egg whites.
9 Pour the mixture into a buttered 23-cm (9-in) round cake tin and bake for 45 min in the centre of the oven.

TIP: Feel free to decorate your cake with icing sugar, flaked almonds and/or grated chocolate.

MATCHA CHOCOLATE COOKIES FROM BOB'S JUICE BAR

MATCHA MAY BE GREEN, BUT IT'S YOUR FRIENDS WHO WILL BE ENVIOUS TO TRY THESE COOKIES. THE FLAVOUR IS BOTH FULL AND CHOCOLATEY, BUT ALSO SUBTLE AND COMPLEX. LIKE MARILYN MONROE, IT'S BOTH BRAINY AND BEAUTIFUL.

Marc Grossman may get more models in Bob's Juice Bar than any fashion house, but this New Yorker in Paris is hunting bigger game. He wants you to eat your veggies. A few years back, the former film-maker hung up his reels and took over a small green space on the rue Lucien Sampaix. He brought in a cactus and a guitar and dubbed it Bob's, the first real juice bar in Paris. And why Bob? 'Because it's easier without my name.'

He does not claim to be leading a revolution, but at his juice bar, the menu based on fruit and vegetables is war cry enough in carnivore-happy Paris. And, scorning Parisian habits, there is no table service – food comes in brown packets, and free tea is offered at the communal table. Somewhere, the rules of the canteen got rewritten.

Sweat Shop is happy to call Marc our guardian angel. He helped us secure the location and coached it into existence. Not a day goes by where we do not say hello, pass a friendly word, raid his shop for smoothies or munch on his heavenly quinoa salad. And, despite his wordy protestations, Marc is cool.

Marc currently runs two restaurants in Paris and is also nursing a burgeoning cookery book empire.

www.bobsjuicebar.com

PREPARATION TIME: 30 min / BAKING TIME: 9 to 13 min

What you need for 20 cookies:

- 400 g (14 oz) plain flour
- 1 tbsp matcha powder
- a pinch of salt
- scant ½ tsp bicarbonate of soda
- 250 g (9 oz) unsalted butter (softened)
- 250 g (9 oz) caster sugar
- 2 eggs
- 250 g (9 oz) plain chocolate (coarsely chopped into large chunks)

Preparation:

1. Mix the flour with the matcha powder, a pinch of salt and the bicarbonate of soda.
2. Whisk the butter and sugar together until creamy.
3. Separate the egg yolks from the whites.
4. Add the yolks to the butter mixture and whisk.
5. Add the butter mixture (wet) to the flour mixture (dry).
6. Beat the egg whites until stiff.
7. Fold the egg whites and chocolate chunks into the batter.
8. Refrigerate the dough for at least 1 hour.
9. Preheat your oven to 220° C (425°F/gas mark 7).
10. Divide the dough into 20 equal parts.
11. Form balls by rolling the dough between your palms and place on non-stick baking trays with enough space between the balls for the cookies to spread out.
12. Place the trays in the oven and lower the temperature to 200° C (400°F/gas mark 6). Bake for 9 to 13 minutes.
13. The cookies should be cooked on the edges but still soft and moist in the middle. They harden as they cool down.

GÉNOISE À LA FRAISE

PREPARATION TIME: 30 min / BAKING TIME: 8 to 10 min

What you need:
- 4 eggs
- 120 g (4¼ oz) granulated sugar, plus 2 tbsp for filling
- a pinch of salt
- 2 tbsp warm water
- finely grated zest of ½ lemon
- 80 g (3 oz) plain flour
- 300 g (10½ oz) strawberries
- 1 tbsp vanilla sugar
- a squeeze of lemon juice
- 200 ml (7 fl oz) whipping cream
- icing sugar (for dusting)

BEES ARE BUZZING LAZILY IN THE GOLDEN LIGHT, FRESH FRUIT ABOUNDS, A BOOK LIES NEGLECTED ON THE LAWN. THIS CAKE IS ALL ABOUT SUMMER. AIRY GÉNOISE GETS THE ROYAL TREATMENT WITH REAL CREAM AND FRESH FRUIT.

Preparation:
1 Preheat your oven to 220° C (425°F/gas mark 7).
2 Separate the egg yolks from the whites.
3 Whisk the egg whites until stiff.
4 Add the larger amount of granulated sugar, the salt and warm water to the egg yolks and whisk until light and foamy.
5 Add the lemon zest.
6 Add the stiffened egg whites to the bowl.
7 Sift the flour slowly into the mix and carefully fold together.
8 Pour the mix into a 30 x 30-cm (12 x 12-in) Swiss roll tin and spread it evenly to 1 cm (⅜ in) in thickness.
9 Bake for 8 to 10 min in the centre of the oven.
10 Leave it to cool.
11 Cut away any dry edges from the sponge, then cut it into three equal pieces.
12 For the filling*, cut the strawberries into small pieces and place them in a bowl. Add the 2 tablespoons of granulated sugar, 1 tablespoon of vanilla sugar and lemon juice. Cover and let stand for a while.
13 Whip the cream and spread half of it on one piece of sponge, add half of the fruit, then repeat with another piece of sponge, the rest of the cream and fruit. Finish by placing the third piece on top.
14 Dust with icing sugar.

*If you're pressed for time, use a simple fruit jam filling.

HOME-MADE SYRUP

PREPARATION TIME: 10 min / ready after 5 days

What you need:
- 1 litre (1¾ pints) water
- 2 kg (4½ lb) sugar
- 40 g (1½ oz) citric acid
- juice of 2 lemons
- fresh herbs such as mint, lemon balm, verbena, elderflowers

Preparation:
1 Boil the water in a large pot and dissolve the sugar and citric acid.
2 Leave the liquid to cool.
3 Add the lemon juice and herbs, put a lid on the pot and stir every second day.
4 After five days, strain and bottle the liquid.

A GORGEOUS, SUNNY DAY IS ALWAYS SWEETER WITH A LITTLE SYRUP. USING FRESH LEAVES FROM THE MARKET OR GARDEN MAKES THIS DELECTABLE SYRUP – WHICH CAN BE USED ON PUDDINGS OR TO ADD SPARKLE TO ANY DRINK – AS ESSENTIAL AS ADDING A BOUQUET OF FLOWERS TO THE DINING TABLE.

NORDIC CARDAMOM BREAD

PREPARATION TIME: 20 min / BAKING TIME: 60 min

What you need:
- 500 g (1 lb 2 oz) soft brown sugar
- 400 ml (14 fl oz) buttermilk
- 2 tsp bicarbonate of soda
- 500 g (1 lb 2 oz) plain flour
- ½ tsp ground cloves
- 1 tsp ground cinnamon
- 1 tsp ground cardamom
- breadcrumbs (for dusting)

THIS LIGHTLY SPICED BUTTERMILK CAKE FROM THE WOOD-FIRED OVENS OF THE NORTH CAN BE EATEN ALL DAY LONG. FOR BREAKFAST HOT FROM THE OVEN WITH BUTTER, OR AS A CAKE TO GO WITH TEA OR COFFEE IN THE AFTERNOON, IT IS A REAL WINTER FAVOURITE. THIS CAKE BRINGS BACK MEMORIES OF NORWEGIAN EVENINGS BY THE FIRE WHEN IT IS COLD AND FROSTY OUTSIDE. PUT ON A JUMPER (WITH REINDEERS OR SNOWFLAKES) AND ENJOY!

Preparation:
1. Preheat your oven to 200°C (400°C/gas mark 6).
2. Mix the sugar into the buttermilk and add the bicarbonate of soda.
3. Sift the flour and spices together.
4. Butter a 24-cm (9½-in) ring cake tin and lightly dust with breadcrumbs. Pour the liquid into the flour mix, stir together and then pour into the cake tin.
5. Bake for 1 hour. Serve hot or cool.

EPISTLE TO A FRIEND

Dear Coffee,

I know that it's been a while since we talked, and perhaps I have never conversed with you, or at least not directly. I know that in your presence I have often praised your fine qualities. But can it be forgivable that I have not acknowledged your generosity in either cruel or clement times? Let me repair this injury.

I draw your attention to one of our venerable trysts...

Your svelte and luscious darkness sat demurely next to a lovely cake in the warmth of a late summer. My friends were chatting amiably about subjects that, once flown, were like vapour in the air. And all the while you kept us company, often facilitating our conversation, our laughter glistening in ripples over your skin. And when we were tired, drifting closer into an afternoon siesta, you sped to our rescue and kissed us sweetly awake.

Dearest friend, all our best and most beautiful moments go largely unheralded, but you have always been at our side. Do not forget our devotion, as we pledge our daily troth to thee.

X

Sweat Shop Top 30

WE DON'T JUST LIKE TO KNIT OR
SEW OR BAKE A CAKE. WE ALSO
LIKE TO DANCE, SING AND JUMP IN
THE AIR! HERE ARE THE SONGS THAT
MAKE SWEAT SHOP'S ROTATION
ON A DAILY BASIS. THINK APRICOT
HIGHLIGHTS IN TOUSLED BLONDE
HAIR OR KISSING THE BOY AND
STEALING HIS DRUMSTICKS.

Paris, You're In Paris – Jimmy Campbell
Last Early Spring – Marie Modiano
Le Cheval en Savon – Valérie Lemercier
Im 80 Stockwerk – Hildegard Knef
The Game – Das Pop
The Free Design – Stereolab
W.E.E.K.E.N.D. – Arling & Cameron
It's Still Rock And Roll To Me – Billy Joel
Brand New Key – Melanie
I Can Buy You – A Camp
Megumi The Milky Way Above – Connan Mockasin
Radar Detector – Darwin Deez
Synchronize – Discodeine
We Can't Fly – Aeroplane
Apple Pie Bed – Lawrence Arabia
Do You Love Me – The Contours
Me Myself And I – De La Soul
Eisbär – Grauzone
Nothing To Worry About – Peter Bjorn & John
Hie Ir Schwyz – Mani Matter
Somebody's Made For Me – Emmitt Rhodes
Il Clan Dei Siciliani – Ennio Morricone
Sweet Virginia – Rolling Stones
Clever Trevor – Ian Dury
Dreams – Fleetwood Mac
Watching The Wheels – John Lennon
Ruin My Day – Jon Brion
Sugar Me – Claudine Longet
Coffee In The Pot – Supergrass
Sunday Mondays – Vanessa Paradis

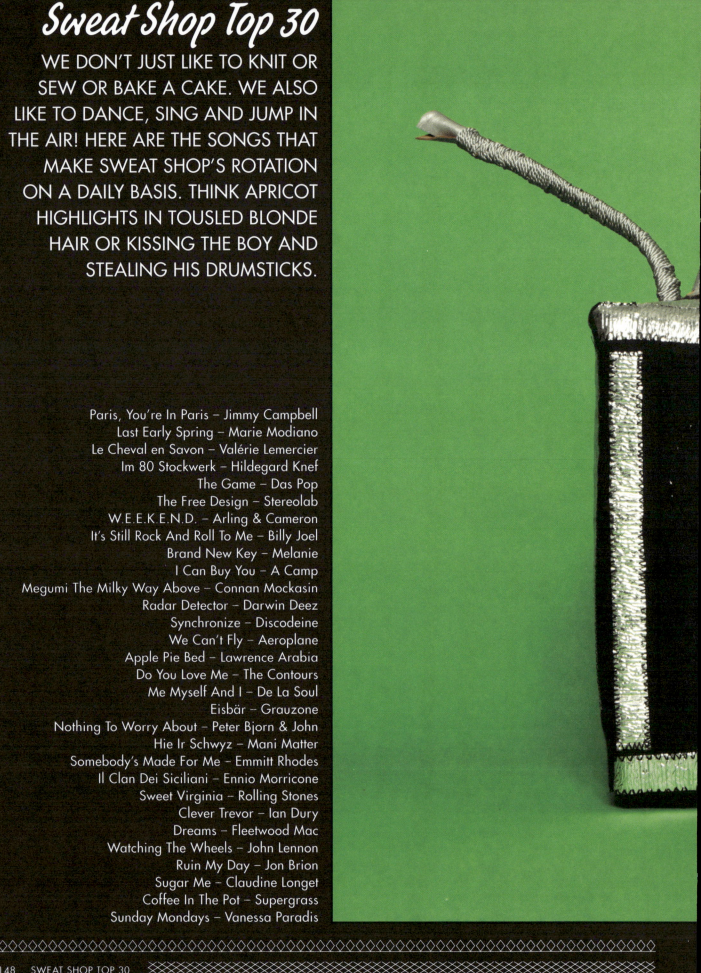

WE REMEMBER WHAT IT WAS LIKE,
POUNDING THE STREETS FOR
BEADED GLASS EYES, HUNGRY
FOR RAMEN OR WONDERING
WHERE TO FIND NICE EARRINGS.
THOSE HOURS WE SPENT ARE
YOURS NOT TO LOSE. THIS LIST
CONTAINS USEFUL ADDRESSES FOR
ALMOST EVERYTHING WE HOLD
DEAR IN PARIS. SO TAKE A LOOK
AT OUR PICKS, GUARANTEED TO
MAKE LIFE EASIER.

FOOD

POZZETTO
39 rue du Roi de Sicile, 75004 Paris
www.pozzetto.biz
Possibly the best ice cream in the city. The milk flavour wows the purists.

BLÉ SUCRÉ
7 Square Trousseau, 75012 Paris
Gorgeous, flaky pastries a few doors down from the café Le Square Trousseau.

BOB'S JUICE BAR
15 rue Lucien Sampaix, 75010 Paris
www.bobsjuicebar.com
Happy, healthy, friendly and good!

BOULANGERIE DU PAIN ET DES IDÉES
34 rue Yves Toudic, 75010 Paris
www.dupainetdesidees.com
Artisanal bread with old-school sourdough starters.

CANDELARIA
52 rue de Saintonge, 75003 Paris
www.candelariaparis.com
Best taqueria this side of the Atlantic. Tostadas, tacos and guacamole to die for. Enjoy mezcal shots in the shack and pass the secret entrance for the speakeasy-style bar.

IZRAEL
30 rue François-Miron, 75004 Paris
A fantastic place to get Mediterranean and North African spices and dried goods. Pricey, but worth going just to see. Closed on Monday.

MARCHÉ DES ENFANTS ROUGE
39, rue de Bretagne, 75003 Paris
Marais weekend hot spot, featuring authentic Japanese bentos and a wide selection of other international brunch fare located in a market.

NANASHI
31 rue de Paradis, 75010 Paris
57 rue Charlot, 75003 Paris
www.31ruedeparadis.com
Parisian Bento with a kitsch '70s French décor. Delicious and informal.

NANIWA
11 rue Sainte-Anne, 75001 Paris
No sushi. Japanese-style canteen with donburis and tayoyaki.

ROSE BAKERY
46 rue Martyr, 75009 Paris
30 rue Debelleyme, 75003 Paris
Famous macrobiotic bakery. Expensive, but delicious and good for you.

ROULEAU DE PRINTEMPS
42, rue Tourtille, 75020 Paris
A lovely family-run Vietnamese restaurant.

BOOKS, FILM, MUSIC, PHOTOGRAPHY

ACTION CINÉMAS
23 rue des Écoles, 5 rue des Écoles, 75005 Paris
4 rue Christine, 75006 Paris
www.actioncinemas.com
The best retro-film cinemas.

ARTAZART
83 quai de Valmy, 75010 Paris
www.artazart.com
Art book shop with great photography and design books.

GROUND ZERO
23 rue Sainte Marthe, 75010 Paris
www.groundzero.fr
Fine selection of records, CDs and books.

LES ARCHIVES DE LA PRESSE
51, rue des Archives, 75003 Paris
www.lesarchivesdelapresse.com
Your one-stop shop for vintage fashion magazines, books, posters and catalogues from the last 50 years. Inspiring.

LOMOGRAPHIE
6 place Franz Liszt, 75010 Paris
17 rue Saint-Croix de la Bretonnerie, 75003 Paris
www.lomography.com
Everything you need for the 4-eyed camera world.

OFR.
20 rue Dupetit-Thouars, 75003 Paris
www.ofrsystem.com
Specialist bookshop with rare fashion and art
magazines.

POTEMKINE DVD STORE
30 rue Beaurepaire, 75010 Paris
www.potemkine.fr
Finely curated selection of DVDs. Expect to see
Criterion and rare art.

THE RED WHEELBARROW BOOKSTORE
22 rue Saint-Paul, 75004 Paris
www.theredwheelbarrow.com
Cute English bookshop.

GALLERIES

GALERIE DU JOUR by Agnés B
44 rue Quincampoix, 75004 Paris
www.galeriedujour.com

GALERIE L.J.
12 rue Commines, 75003 Paris
www.galerielj.com

GALERIE THADDAEUS ROPAC
7 rue Debelleyme, 75003 Paris
www.ropac.net

MAISON ROUGE
10 boulevard de la Bastille, 75012 Bastille
www.lamaisonrouge.org

MUSÉE DE LA VIE ROMANTIQUE
16 rue Chaptal, 75009 Paris
Art collection and objects from nineteenth-century
writer George Sand and painter Ary Scheffer. Known
for its delightful teatime in the garden (open from May
to September) where you can listen to readings or
little concerts.

PALAIS DE TOKYO
13 avenue du President Wilson, 75016 Paris
www.palaisdetokyo.com
Art gallery, museum, bookshop, gadget shop,
restaurant and hang-out all in one place. Cross
the street to check out the fashion museum.

THE LAZY DOG
25 rue de Charonne, 75011 Paris
www.thelazydog.fr

WORKSHOPS

ATELIER MYRIAGONE
16 avenue Desgenettes, 94100 Saint Maur des Fossés
www.atelier-myriagone.fr
DIY screen-printing at 10EU/H.

ATELIER NIKOLAS SERDAR
17 rue La Vieuville, 75018 Paris
www.serdart.com
Workshops in printmaking, drawing and
screen-printing.

CRAFT SHOPS

ENTRÉE DES FOURNISSEURS
8 rue des Francs Bourgeois, 75003 Paris
www.entreedesfournisseurs.fr
Haberdashery.

FIL2000
65 rue Réaumur, 75002 Paris
Best prices for needles, thread and general sewing
supplies. Also known as 'The Closet'.

FLORENT ROINA
73 rue Charlot, 75003 Paris
Buttonholes, poppers and covered buttons for last-
minute tweaking.

LA DROGUERIE
9–11 rue du Jour, 75001 Paris
www.ladroguerie.com
The poshest jungle for beautiful sewing supplies.

MOKUBA
18 rue Montmartre, 75001 Paris
www.mokuba.fr
Ribbons galore!

SOCOLATEX
12 rue du Bourg L'Abée, 75003 Paris
Geared towards professionals.

FABRIC SHOPS

AU BONHEUR DES DAMES
1–3 rue Livingstone, 75018 Paris
Cheap pre-cut bolts of fabric.

CUIRS CHADEFAUX
18 rue Taylor, 75010 Paris
www.cuirschadefaux.com
Leather supplier. Expensive but good. Cheap scraps
for bargain hunters.

DE GILLES TISSUS
156 rue de la Roquette, 75011 Paris
www.degilles.com
High-end fabric paradise, with even vintage fabric
from the '20s.

MARCHÉ SAINT-PIERRE
2 rue Charles Nodier, 75018 Paris
www.marchesaintpierre.com
A patchwork of little fabric shops and mercerizes.

MAUPIOU
2 rue de la paix, 75002 Paris
www.maupiou.com
Old-school French fabric shop. Glamour.

WWW.MOTIFPERSONNEL.COM
Order your own fabric design per metre. (22EU/m)

POULAIN PEAUSSERIE
52 boulevard Richard Lenoir, 75011 Paris
www.peausseriepoulain.com
Leather in myriad colours. One sheep 40EU.

RUE HEROLD
8 rue Herold, 75001 Paris
www.rueherold.com
Upholstery fabric.

TISSUS REINE
3–5 place Saint-Pierre, 75018 Paris
www.tissus-reine.com
Huge selection of fabric.

IE
128 rue Vieille du Temple, 75003 Paris
Vintage children's clothing and fabric inspired by
The Arabian Nights.

BOISSON ET CIE
181 rue Saint Denis, 75002 Paris
Wide selection of yarn.

PIERRE HUGUET ET CIE ETC
36 rue Réaumur, 75003 Paris
Beautiful yarns.

FLEA MARKETS

BELLEVILLE STREET MARKET
Boulevard de Belleville, between Metros Couronnes
and Belleville, 75019 Paris
Fly-by-night market that pops up on weekends
unexpectedly. A bit of a rubbish heap, so come
prepared.

CAR BOOT SALES
Garage sales and nonprofessional vendors selling
clothing, furniture, accessories.
Online calender: http://vide-greniers.org

MARCHÉ D'ALIGRE
Place d'Aligre, 75011 Paris
http://marchedaligre.free.fr
Cute daily market (every day except Monday) with
flowers, food, clothes and furniture. Great neighbourhood known for its May '68 residents.

PORTE DE VANVES
Avenue Marc Sangnier et avenue Georges Lafenestre,
75014 Paris
Saturdays and Sundays.
Attention! Only mornings: 7 a.m. to 1 p.m.
Fantastic market for antlers.

PUCES DE MONTREUIL
Porte de Montreuil, 75020 Paris
Good flea market for old books, sunglasses, boots and
furniture.

PUCES DE ST. OUEN / PORTE DE CLIGNANCOURT
Porte de Clignancourt, 75018 Paris
Saturdays to Mondays, all day.
One of the most established flea markets in the city.

VINTAGE

AUX COMPTOIR DU CHINEUR
49 rue Saint-Paul, 75004 Paris
Chaotic and mad vintage shop run by the excellent Laurent featuring retro objects, records, boots, telephones, roller skates and novelty sunglasses.

CROIX ROUGE
40 rue Albert Thomas, 75010 Paris
Shhhhh… Where we sneak off during breaks to raid for mad and fun clothing.

DIDIER LUDOT
20–24 Galerie Montpensier, 75001 Paris
www.didierludot.fr
Legendary vintage *haute couture* where celebrities shop. Exclusive and expensive.

EMMAUS
22 boulevard Beaumarchais, 75004 Paris
54 rue de Charonne, 75011 Paris
80 boulevard Jourdon, 75014 Paris
105 boulevard Davout, 75020 Paris
340 rue des Pyrénées, 75020 Paris
www.emmaus-france.org
Charity vintage shop, which also sells furniture.

GUERRISOL
29–31 avenue de Clichy, 75017 Paris
96 boulevard Barbès, 75018 Paris
17 boulevard de Rochechouart, 75009 Paris
17 boulevard de la Chapelle, 75010 Paris
A Paris classic for vintage bargain hunters. Sift through the massive selection of used clothing. Cheap fur coats.

JUPON ROUGE
19, rue de Rochechouart, 75009 Paris

LABRUSSE
26 boulevard de Magenta, 75010 Paris
Vintage wood furniture.

LA CAVERNE À FRIPES
25 rue Houdon, 75018 Paris

LA JOLIE GARDE-ROBE
15 rue Commines, 75003 Paris

MAMZ'ELLE SWING
35 rue Roi de Sicile, 75004 Paris
Time travel to the wonderful world of Zazou.

MON AMOUR
77 rue Charlot, 75003 Paris
Sandrine and Narumi offer a cool collection of '70s and '80s vintage pieces. Also lightly worn designer clothes from recent seasons.

THANX GOD I'M A V.I.P.
12 rue de Lancry, 75010 Paris
www.thanxgod.com

CLOTHING & ACCESSORIES

ANDREA CREWS
25 rue de Vaucouleurs, 75011 Paris
www.andreacrews.com
Pop fashion label with a colourful DIY look run by international artist Maroussia.

CAILLES DE LUXE
15 rue Keller, 75011 Paris
www.caillesdeluxe.com
Handmade goodies that are perfect for birthdays.

CULOTTE
7 rue Malher, 75004 Paris
www.poidsnetparis.com
Pretty jewellery by a young Japanese designer.

LA BOTICA
89 rue de Bagnolet, 75020 Paris
www.labotica.fr
Laboratory of young designers.

PUBLIC ROMANCE
153 rue Amelot, 75011 Paris
www.publicromance.com
Cool and nicely priced young designers as well as a nice selection of vintage pieces.

RENÉ TALMON L'ARMÉE
3 rue Cunin Gridaine, 75003 Paris
www.renetalmonlarmee.com
Stunning, well-made jewellery.

Notes

GLOSSARY

A

APPLIQUÉ
A type of ornamentation, as a cut-out design, that is sewn on to or otherwise applied to a piece of fabric or material.

B

BASTING
Loose stitches to hold material in place for the final sewing.

BIAS
An oblique or diagonal line of direction across woven fabric.

BIAS BINDING
A strip of material cut on the bias for extra stretch and often doubled, used for binding hems, seams, interfacings or for decoration.

BINDING
A strip of material that protects or decorates the edges of fabric.

BLIND HEMMING
Specific hemming stitch that is invisible from the visible side of the garment.

BOURDON STITCHING
A decorative satin stitch.

C

CLIP
A small cut at the edge (2 mm/¹⁄₁₆ in) of the fabric used to indicate a pattern marking such as a fold line, centre front line or dart position.

D

DARNING
To mend any garment or anything sewn with rows of stitches, sometimes by crossing and interweaving rows to span a gap.

DRAPE
The way the fabric falls.

E

EDGE STITCHING
A straight stitch running along the edge of a fabric, usually about 1mm (¹⁄₃₂ in) from the edge of the fabric. Edge stitching is often visible.

EMBROIDERY
The art of stitching ornamental designs into material using threads of silk, cotton, gold, silver or other material.

F

FACING
A lining or material applied to fabric for strengthening or ornamentation.

FUSIBLE MATERIALS: FUSIBLE CANVAS, FUSIBLE TAPE
A thin layer of material with heat-activated adhesive used to strengthen or stiffen fabric.

G

GATHER
To draw fabric into fine folds or puckers by means of even stitches.

GRAIN
The direction of threads in any woven fabric in relation to the selvage.

H

HEM
An edge made by folding back the edges of the fabric and using small stitches to hold in place.

HEMMING TAPE
Adhesive tape, usually heat activated, slipped inside the edge and used in place of hemming.

I

INTERFACING
A woven or non-woven material used between the facing and outer fabric to give support and shape. Interfacing is often used in collars and lapels to fix their shape.

INTERLINING
An inner lining or wadding placed between the ordinary lining and the outer fabric, often for volume or warmth. The best example of this is cotton or wool used in quilting.

INVISIBLE STITCHING
Stitching that is invisible from the right side of the fabric; done either by machine with a special foot or by hand.

J

JERSEY
A machine-made, fine-knit fabric of wool, silk, nylon, rayon, etc., characteristically soft and elastic, primarily used for garments.

L

LACE
A netlike ornament made by crocheted or knitted threads. Can be hand or machine made.

LINING
A fabric sewn inside the garment, usually made of lighter-weight material, and used to finish the garment or give opacity to sheer fabrics.

M

MUSLIN
A fairly thin fabric made with loosely woven cotton. Can be used for making patterns, and is often used in upholstery and curtains. Very breathable.

N

NOTCH
An angular or V-shaped cut made on the outside of a stitched curve.

O

OVERLOCK STITCH
A stitch that is sewn over the edge of one or two pieces of fabric for edging, hemming or seaming.

P

PATCHWORK
Work made from sewing together cut blocks of cloth or leather of various colours or shapes. Used particularly in quilting.

PATTERN
Template for the construction of a garment or anything sewn, and usually printed on paper. The pattern is usually traced or pinned on to the fabric and cut out.

PLEATS
Folds of definite, even width made by doubling material on itself and stitching it in place.

R

RAW EDGE
The cut edge of a piece of garment before it is finished or hemmed.

RIGHT SIDE
The part of the garment that is visible when finished.

RUNNING STITCH
A sewing stitch made by passing the needle in and out in a line with short, even stitches.

S

SADDLE STITCH
An oversewn stitch, especially one made with a strip of leather or a thick leather-like cord, used in saddle making and other leather work.

SATIN STITCH
A long, straight embroidery stitch consisting of parallel rows stitched closely together to form a surface that resembles satin.

SEAM ALLOWANCE
The area between the edge of the fabric and the stitching line on two (or more) pieces of material being stitched together.

SEAM LINE
The line where two or more layers of material are being held together by stitches.

SELVAGE
The finished edge of woven fabric that prevents unravelling. The selvage often looks like a narrow tape and is visibly separate from the woven part of the fabric.

SEWING
To join or attach by running thread through material and knotting. Can refer to both hand sewing or machine stitching.

SHIRRING
To draw up or gather material on three or more parallel threads.

SLASH
A cut opening in any garment. Can be for pockets or for inserting contrasting piping.

STABILIZERS
Used to stabilize a fabric for such things as machine embroidery and buttonhole sewing. They prevent the fabric stretching and distorting while the process is carried out.

STITCHING
Any series of stitches made by a sewing machine.

T

TOPSTITCHING
A decorative stitch like edge stitching, but usually around 6 mm (¼ in) from the edge.

W

WARP
The set of threads placed lengthways in the loom, crossed by and interlaced with the weft, and forming the lengthways threads in any woven fabric. Stronger than the weft, which is why almost all garments are cut along the warp (i.e., on the grain).

WEFT
Also called the woof, these are the threads woven across the width of the fabric, running through the lengthways warp.

WRONG SIDE
The hidden side of the finished garment or sewn piece.

INDEX

A

album cover knits 86–9
almond–chocolate cake 141
Arabian skort 30–5
Artazart 14, 17, 152
Ayada, Momo 124

B

bags
    banana 62–3
    shopping 24–5, 58–61
balaclava 90–1
balls 130–1
banana bag 62–3
bead weaving 108–11
Bob's Juice Bar 14, 15, 17,
    142, 152
body measurement 27
bonbon 114–17
bootie 72–5
Bordarier, Cyril 16
Boulangerie du Pain et des
    Idées 14, 15, 17, 152

C

café couture 10
cape 100–3
cardamom bread 146
Chez Chiffons 14, 16, 17
chocolate cake
    almond 141
    Martena's 141
    Sissi's 140
chocolate cookie 142–3
Christmas ornament 76–7
Cinquante, Le 14, 16, 17
coffee 147
crochet jumper 96–7

D

David Bowie knits 86, 88, 89
Davidtelevision, Sébastien
    86–9
Doczekalski, Sandrine 64–9
draught blocker 114–17
dress
    tulip 54–7
Dudu, Vava 108–11
Dupuy, Céline 38–41

F

fabric making 98–9
Fair Isle knitting 87
family heads Christmas
    baubles 76–7
finger puppets 92–3
fishnet jumper 80–1
flapper trousers 64–9
Flash Gordon 92–3
flowerpot cosy 126–7
footwear
    customizing shoes 106–7
    house bootie 72–5
    house socks 82–3

G

génoise à la fraise 144
Grossman, Marc 15, 142–3

H

hat 38–41
home-made syrup 145
hoodie 42–5
Horsting, Viktor 100
house bootie 72–5
house socks 82–3

I

intarsia knitting 87, 90–1

J

jacket
    motorcycle 108–11
    Todti's 46–53
    va-va-voom 108–11
Jade's collection 70–1
jeans mask 118–23
jumpers
    album covers 86–9
    crochet 96–7
    fishnet 80–1
    with a theme 86–9
jumper with a theme 86–9

K

Karaly, Hubert 14, 16, 17
knitted snake 84–5

L

leather
    paint 60, 106
    plaiting 133
    sewing 59, 61
    soles 74
    straps 60–1
    weaving 132
Lerch, Carolin 26–9
loop knitting 134–5

M

magic plait, the 133
make your own fabric 98–9
Martena, the 38–41
mask
    jeans 118–23
    sleeping 104–5
matcha chocolate cookie
    142–3
measuring 27
Médecine Douce 14, 17
Mille, Delphine 118–23
Mlle Kou 38–41
Momo le Moins Cher 14, 15,
    17
motorcycle jacket 108–11

N

Nordic cardamom bread 146

O

O'Mara, Madison 92–3

P

pattern making 26–9
Pelican Avenue 26–9
Pepijn 124
plaid-blanket cape 100–3
plaiting 133

Q

quick-knit fishnet jumper 80–1

S

sewing tools 36–7
shoes, customizing 106–7
shopping bag 24–5, 58–61
Simons, Raf 58
skort 30–5
sleeping mask 104–5
snake 84–5
socks 82–3
songs 148
Sonia Rykiel 64
stranding 87
Studio Berçot 46
syrup 145

T

T-shirt pattern 26–9
Tanker's Wall 124–5
10th arrondissement 7
    history 12–13
    map 14
    the neighbourhood 15–17
themed jumpers 86–9
Threads 136–7
Thrun, Isabell 42–5, 136
Todtenbier, Jörg 46–53
tools 36–7
Towers, Emily 126–7
trousers
    flapper 64–9
tulip dress 54–7
twisted hoodie 42–5

V

van Looy, Floris 124
va-va-voom jacket 108–11
Velthuis, Hester 100–3
Verheyden, Michaël 58–61
Verre Volé, Le 14, 16, 17
vintage wall 124–5

W

wall of fame 18–19
wallpaper 124–5
weaving leather 132

Y

yarn making 126–7

Z

Zampetti, Delphine 16
Zweite Haut 46